A Woman's Journey to the Heart of God

Also by Cynthia Heald

Becoming a Woman of Excellence (1986, NavPress)
Intimacy with God Through the Psalms (1987, NavPress)
Loving Your Husband (1989, NavPress)
Loving Your Wife, with Jack Heald (1989, NavPress)
Becoming a Woman of Freedom (1992, NavPress)
Becoming a Woman of Purpose (1994, NavPress)
Abiding in Christ: A Month of Devotionals (1995, NavPress)
Becoming a Woman of Prayer (1996, NavPress)

A Woman's Journey to the Heart of God

Cynthia Heald

OLIVER NELSON

THOMAS NELSON PUBLISHERS
Nashville • Atlanta • London • Vancouver

Published in Nashville, Tennessee, by Thomas Nelson, Inc., Publishers, and distributed in Canada by Word Communications, Ltd., Richmond, British Columbia.

Published in association with the literary agency of Alive Communications, 1465 Kelly Johnson Blvd., Suite #320, Colorado Springs, CO 80920.

The material credited to Amy Carmichael is taken from *IF* by Amy Carmichael. Copyright © 1980 by The Zondervan Corporation. Used by permission of Zondervan Publishing House.

The material credited to Oswald Chambers is taken from *My Utmost for His Highest* by Oswald Chambers. Copyright © 1935 by Dodd Mead & Co., renewed © 1963 by the Oswald Chambers Publications Assn. Ltd., and is used by permission of Discovery House Publishers, Box 3566, Grand Rapids, MI 49501. All rights reserved.

Scripture quotations noted AMPLIFIED are from THE AMPLIFIED BIBLE: Old Testament. Copyright © 1962, 1964 by Zondervan Publishing House (used by permission); and from THE AMPLIFIED NEW TESTAMENT. Copyright © 1958 by the Lockman Foundation (used by permission).

Scripture quotations noted *The Message* are from *The Message: The New Testament in Contemporary English*. Copyright © 1993 by Eugene H. Peterson.

Scripture quotations noted MOFFATT are from *The Bible: James Moffatt Translation* by James A. R. Moffatt. Copyright © 1922, 1924, 1925, 1926, 1935 by HarperCollins San Francisco. Copyright 1950, 1952, 1953, 1954 by James A. R. Moffatt.

Scripture quotations noted NASB are taken from the NEW AMERICAN STANDARD BIBLE ®. © Copyright The Lockman Foundation 1960, 1962, 1963, 1968, 1971, 1972, 1973, 1975, 1977. Used by permission.

Scripture quotations noted NLT are taken from the *Holy Bible,* New Living Translation, copyright © 1996. Used by permission of Tyndale House Publishers, Inc., Wheaton, Illinois 60189. All rights reserved.

Scripture quotations noted PHILLIPS are from J. B. Phillips: THE NEW TESTAMENT IN MODERN ENGLISH. Revised Edition. Copyright © J. B. Phillips 1958, 1960, 1972. Used by permission of Macmillan Publishing Co., Inc.

Scripture quotations noted WILLIAMS are from *The New Testament in the Language of the People* by Charles B. Williams. © Copyright 1986 by Holman Bible Publishers. All rights reserved.

Library of Congress Cataloging-in-Publication Data

Heald, Cynthia.
   A woman's journey to the heart of God / Cynthia Heald.
     p. cm.
   Includes bibliographical references.
   ISBN 0-7852-7239-9
   1. Christian women—Religious life.   I.Title.
BV4527.H42   1997
248.8'43—dc21

97–17803
CIP

Printed in the United States of America.

1 2 3 4 5 6 BVG 02 01 00 99 98 97

To
Jack
God's gracious gift to accompany me on my journey—
I would want no one else to carry my bags.

Happy are those who are strong in the LORD,
   who set their minds on a pilgrimage to Jerusalem.
When they walk through the Valley of Weeping,
   it will become a place of refreshing springs,
   where pools of blessing collect after the rains!
They will continue to grow stronger,
   and each of them will appear before God in Jerusalem.

Psalm 84:5–7 NLT

Contents

Section Three: Enjoying the Journey

Acknowledgments

I was always told that writing a book was like giving birth, but I discovered that there is no pregnancy—one goes immediately into hard labor until the book is done! There are many who "coached" me through my labor, and it is a privilege to thank them publicly.

Victor Oliver—this book would not have been written without your vision, prayers, encouragement, guidance—and delicious pears.

Kathy Yanni—how I thank the Lord for bringing us together for tea thirteen years ago. My life has never been the same! (I'm afraid yours changed too!) You are much more than an editor or agent to me—you are a dear daughter in the Lord. Your love, prayers, and encouragement have continually blessed my life in so many ways. Thanks for always maintaining my integrity, for your amazing ability to make my writing readable and much more interesting, and for your wonderful sense of humor. I would not ever want to write without you.

Jack—thanks for the countless cups of tea, the tissues for my tears, and the War Wanton Soup. Your prayers with me and your encouraging counsel were special evidences of your love.

Melinda & Mark, Daryl & Cathy, Shelly & Lianchao, & Michael— my precious children who have called, prayed, and taught me so much. I would not have anything to write about without you!

My dear friends—the Lord has blessed me with friends who allow me to drop in and out of their lives at my convenience—either physically or by mail. How I thank Him for each of you faithfully upholding me in prayer. There were many days when your prayers made all the difference. Thank you for co-"laboring" with me.

Of course, without the Lord we can do nothing—Lord, my heart overflows with gratitude for the honor I have had to sit at Your feet, listen to Your voice, and sense Your presence as I have attempted to put into words what it is like to journey to Your heart. Thank You for using this book to change my life and to bring me closer to Your heart. Thank You for letting me be Your child.

Preface

Going on a journey to an unknown destination can be appealing, but also a little bewildering. What is it like to go on this trip? What do I need to pack? What will the weather be like? We want to talk with someone who has already been there so we will know what to expect.

I have never considered myself a travel guide, but here I am writing a handbook for our journey to the heart of God. I have been on this journey for many years, and it is a delight to share some of my experiences, tell you how to pack, answer questions about the destination, and let you know about the conditions along the way.

We travel a well-trodden path, in the footsteps of past seekers of God. In the Psalms there is a songbook called the Song of Ascents. Psalms 120–34 are the songs the Hebrew pilgrims sang as they traveled to Jerusalem. Since these ancient wayfarers sang on their journey, I thought that a hymn at the end of each chapter would be appropriate for us as we journey toward the heart of God.

You will also find questions placed throughout each chapter. They are intended to give you opportunity for pausing along the way—to reflect on your responses, to pray about what the Lord is bringing to your attention, or perhaps to write down something you want to remember or a commitment you want to make.

Concerning books, Oswald Chambers had these thoughts: "The author who benefits you most is not the one who tells you something you did not know before, but the one who gives expression to the truth that has been dumbly struggling in you for utterance."[1]

My prayer is that, in some way, I will be able to express truth that will penetrate your heart and enable you to rejoice in your pilgrimage, persevere

in all kinds of weather, and be richly blessed and transformed as you journey to the dear heart of our Father.

Love in Christ,
Cynthia Heald

THE FATHER
AND THE CHILD

The Father spoke:

Come, child, let us journey together.

Where shall we go, Father?

To a distant land, another kingdom.

So the journey will be long?

Yes, we must travel every day.

When will we reach our destination?

At the end of your days.

And who will accompany us?

Joy and Sorrow.

Must Sorrow travel with us?

Yes, she is necessary to keep you close to Me.

But I want only Joy.

It is only with Sorrow that you will know
true Joy.

What must I bring?

A willing heart to follow Me.

What shall I do on the journey?

There is only one thing that you must do—
stay close to Me. Let nothing distract you.
Always keep your eyes on Me.

And what will I see?

You will see My glory.

And what will I know?

You will know My heart.

The Father stretched out His hand.

The child, knowing the great love her Father had
for her, placed her hand in His and began her
journey.

Preparing for a Lifetime Journey

The impulse to pursue God originates with God, but the outworking of that impulse is our following hard after Him. All the time we are pursuing Him we are already in His hand.

A. W. Tozer[1]

The highest privilege and greatest joy I have had in my life is to journey toward the heart of our Father. His desire to lead me to places I would never dare to go has deeply enriched and shaped my life. A major part of my journey is now over, and as I look back, I am humbled by His tender care and personal involvement in my life. I cherish the day I placed my hand in His. My journey is His journey, and it has given me a priceless glimpse of His heart.

We are all on a journey through life. I have found that choosing to travel toward the eternal provides a needed anchor in today's world. Many destinations clamor for our attention. With so many "pulls" on our time and identity, it can be difficult to discern which road to travel each day. But choose we must, for each day takes us toward some destination. In the following chapters, we will explore what is needed—and the riches that await us—when we choose to follow hard after God's heart.

Getting Ready

Have you ever decided to undertake an extended journey? If so, you know that once you begin to plan, there will be much excitement and anticipation. You tell your friends; you read about your destination; your thoughts are continually preoccupied with everything that must be accomplished and all that must be packed before you can actually depart. Even in the midst of your normal routines, your focus is always drawn to your impending travel. You expend a lot of energy just in getting ready to go!

At times my "getting ready" was so monumental that I was exhausted by the day of departure. I remember reading about a dear woman who became overwhelmed with all that needed to be done before she left on a trip. In exasperation she went to her husband and declared, "I can get ready to go, or I can go; but I can't do both!"

With so many "pulls" on our time and identity, it can be difficult to discern which road to travel each day.

Certainly, going on a trip can become a burden when we have to make preparations while we are still trying to maintain the responsibilities of our lives from day to day. We may find ourselves shrinking from some adventures because we know the high cost that such a commitment demands.

"Is there anything in your life that is hindering you from choosing to follow hard after God's heart?"

When my husband, Jack, and I were newly arrived in Temple, Texas, I was six months pregnant with our third child. Melinda was two and a half years old; Daryl was eight months. Jack had just bought a veterinary clinic. One day he shared that he wanted to go to Dallas to be with some missionaries he had met in Korea when he was in the air force. Since his return from Korea he had made a commitment to follow Christ, and he wanted to tell his friends of their influence and of his decision. What a wonderful idea! I encouraged him to go.

Jack wanted me to go with him, but he didn't think we should take our small children. Not take our children! We knew no one who could keep them, and I was more than willing to stay home. Leaving our children would be too high a cost, I thought. No, I would not go. I would not be with my husband as he spent time with the people who meant so much to him. I would just have to miss out on that special time in his life.

It turns out I went to Dallas. A woman from the church we were visiting stayed with Melinda and Daryl—who survived the experience and are now healthy, secure adults! I was able to be with Jack as he shared his newfound faith. Because I went, he knew that my journey was with him, and I was blessed in the process. If I had continued to think, *No, this is impossible, I cannot leave,* I would have missed experiencing God's provision of a sitter, time away with my husband, and the enrichment of being with godly men and women. I was willing to go to Dallas because I knew it was a worthy trip.

Motivation to count the cost in preparing for a trip is often determined by the destination. Certainly, knowing God, desiring His plan, and experiencing His presence have value, worth, and purpose that can be found on no other road. Are you fearful of what the preparation might require for your journey with God? Don't let it keep you from receiving the benefits of His care, His blessing, and His desire for you to trust in Him.

One Day at a Time

This world, full of wickedness, is a harsh place to live. We need a destination that will allow us to travel a different path toward a righteous, safe, eternal dwelling. Deuteronomy 33:26–27 tells us there is "no God like the God of Jeshurun, who rides through heaven to your rescue, sublimely through the skies! God eternal is your home, and underneath are the ever-lasting arms!" (MOFFATT).

God eternal is our home, and He invites us to journey toward His heart. He sent His only Son to purchase us and to prepare a place for us. The opportunity to travel to this destination came at great expense. Any sacrifice to go on this journey will be honored.

> *Each day becomes precious because each day is part of the process that takes us nearer to the heart of God.*

Yet a decision to journey toward His heart brings uncertainty, for the destination is shrouded in mystery. It raises questions: Am I *ready* for such an important expedition? Am I properly prepared? Do I have suitable clothes? Do I have to learn a new language? Do I have the right road map? I can't go until everything is in place!

The word *journey* originally meant a march of just one day. A *journeyman* meant a worker by the day; a *journal,* a daily record. Once we understand that the journey *begins* with our commitment to travel toward the heart of God, we can be free of the fear of being unprepared. Each day becomes precious because each day is part of the process that takes us nearer to the heart of God. Then all the preparation and sacrifice necessary to arrive at our destination take on new meaning.

How often I say, "Tomorrow I will be more consistent in prayer; next week I will study more." I so easily forget that each day is part of my journey. My journey to the heart of God does not begin tomorrow; the choices I make today determine whether I move toward Him, or toward self and the world.

William Law cautioned us, "Don't please yourself with thinking how piously you would act and submit to God in a plague, a famine, or persecution, but be intent upon the perfection of the present day, and be assured that the best way of showing true zeal is to make little things the occasions of great piety."[2]

> *"Where are you on your journey— waiting to begin, or traveling day by day?"*

Picture a restless young man. His life is too tidy, too narrow. He asks his father for his inheritance, and he takes off on his own journey. He travels far away from his father's home and heart.

The young man is free to live his own life now. He no longer has to ask his father's permission for any actions he wants to take. At first, it is freeing to wake up in the morning and do whatever he wants, with no accountability to anyone. But after a period of time, his poor choices begin to affect his carefree lifestyle. To make things worse, there is famine in the land. He finds himself not only feeding swine, but also eating with them. His journey, shaped by his daily decisions, has led him to a bitter place. He realizes that he would be better off as his father's servant, and so he returns to his father, who readily embraces him.

> *The choices I make today determine whether I move toward Him, or toward self and the world.*

You may never wake up one day and act on a rash impulse to head out of town for the pleasures of the far country. But your daily choices will set you on a certain course. Each day becomes essential in determining which direction your life will take.

Don't Wait Until Tomorrow

For some reason I think that everything has to be in order in my life if I am to walk with God. I imagine that all decisions will have been made and I will be all packed. And I will no longer have much responsibility for other things because I'll be leaving on my journey!

I wonder how often we postpone our walk with God until life seems a little more under control. "When I don't have to work so hard . . . when the children are in school . . . when my parents are better . . . when I have more time . . . *then* I will begin my journey." How tragic to go through life without realizing that our walk toward God's heart is a daily journey. We cannot make up for lost time. We can never recover yesterday.

In this light, Jesus' words become fresh: "If anyone wishes to come after Me, let him deny himself, and take up his cross *daily,* and follow Me" (Luke 9:23 NASB, italics added). Our walk with the Lord is a daily commitment to identify with Jesus.

> *Your journey begins the minute you say, "Yes, I want to walk with my God, and I will trust Him for each day of my life."*

Knowing this is freeing to me. I don't have to be perfect. I don't have to have all the spiritual disciplines in place. If I am willing to follow Christ, then each day becomes a time of preparation. Each day, no matter what it brings, is part of the process of my journey to God's heart.

Yet sometimes the very dailiness of this process can discourage us. We feel that we're not making any spiritual progress. We see no growth or ministry or significant service.

Before I began to serve in public ministry, I was a wife and mother of four for twenty-seven years. I led Bible studies, and I desired to be as consistent as I could be in spending time with the Lord each day, but I spent the majority of my days cooking, washing, and driving! I remember a young mother of three boys asking me, "All I do is cook, clean, and go to soccer games—is that enough?" The answer is yes! Even though we do not sense that we are doing anything profound for God, it is important to understand that God continually works in the daily circumstances of our lives. Our part is not to look at our situation, but to set our hearts to draw near to our heavenly Father. Our circumstances should not dictate when we begin our journey.

"Are you focused on the dailiness of your walk with God?"

In the Sermon on the Mount, Jesus seemed intent on teaching us to let go of worrying about how things will turn out:

> So don't worry about having enough food or drink or clothing. Why be like the pagans who are so deeply concerned about these things? Your heavenly Father already knows all your needs, and he will give you all you need from day to day if you live for him and

make the Kingdom of God your primary concern. So don't worry about tomorrow, for tomorrow will bring its own worries. Today's trouble is enough for today. (Matt. 6:31–34 NLT)

The Lord addressed our concern for our physical needs, but He emphasized the primacy of seeking His kingdom and living one day at a time.

"How did you receive your call to speak and write?" someone once asked me. That question had never before been posed to me, and my first thought was, *Well, actually, I have not received a call to this ministry!* As I reflected, however, I realized that years ago I had discerned God's call in His invitation, "Come, follow Me and walk with Me daily."

And so His call goes to all who respond to Him, "Come, the best journey you can have in this world is the one into My heart." Your journey begins the minute you say, "Yes, I want to walk with my God, and I will trust Him for each day of my life."

❦❦

"It is easy to imagine that we will get to a place where we are complete and ready, but preparation is not suddenly accomplished," advised Oswald Chambers. "It is a process steadily maintained."[3]

Undertaking a lifetime journey is indeed a process, filled with excitement and anticipation but also apprehension. Committing to go will raise many questions:

- *What do I need?*
- *What should I leave behind?*
- *What will happen along the way?*
- *What are the most important things to see?*
- *What will it be like when I reach the destination?*
- *Is the trip truly worth taking?*

Dear friend, if these are some of your questions, please read on. We're going on a five-star journey with priceless experiences along the way and an eternal destination awaiting us. You need not complete your preparations ahead of time in order to come along. All you need to be ready for this journey is the willingness to take your Father's outstretched hand.

Jesus calls us o'er the tumult
Of our life's wild, restless sea;
Day by day I hear Him saying,
"Christian, come and follow me."[4]

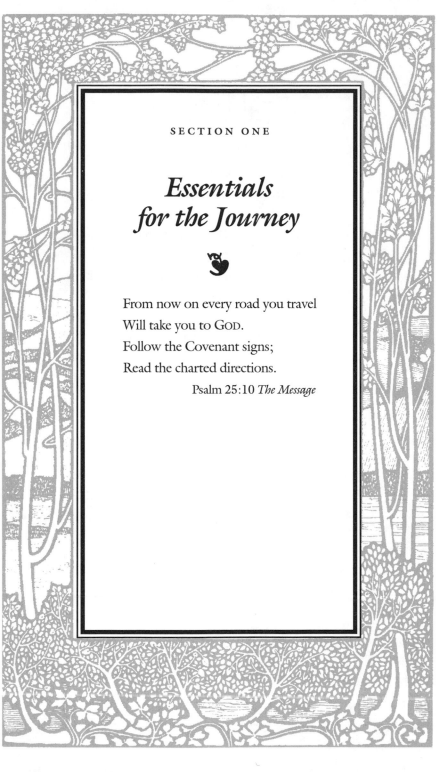

SECTION ONE

Essentials for the Journey

From now on every road you travel
Will take you to GOD.
Follow the Covenant signs;
Read the charted directions.

Psalm 25:10 *The Message*

THE FATHER
AND THE CHILD

The Father spoke:

Are you ready, My child?

Yes, but I have nothing to bring except myself.

You are all I need.

Surely I must bring something; I do not feel prepared to travel.

Do not concern yourself with preparations. Your journey has already begun.

But I am fearful.

There is no need to fear; I will always be with you.

Will You give me what I need?

I will provide for you.

What will You provide?

All that is essential for your journey.

And what is essential?

I will show you along the way. For now, you have what is necessary: the desire to draw close to My heart.

TWO

An
Invitation

> Now over the gate there was written: "Knock, and it shall be opened unto you" (Matt. 7:7). He knocked, therefore, more than once or twice, saying, "May I now enter here?"...
>
> *Christian:* "Here is a poor burdened sinner. I come from the City of Destruction, but am going to Mount Zion, that I may be delivered from the wrath to come: I would therefore, sir, since I am informed that by this gate is the way thither, know if you are willing to let me in."
>
> *Goodwill:* "I am willing with all my heart."
>
> And with that he opened the gate.[1]

An invitation arrives, requesting that you go on a life-changing journey. You feel special to have been asked, but the invitation sounds rather vague. It is for you alone, and it asks for implicit faith in the Guide, whom you will never see. You have no say in the itinerary or the mode of travel. You do have the Guide's promise of an incredible gift and the assurance of His continual presence with you along the way.

As you look more closely at the enclosed brochure, you discover that no payment is required of you—this trip is free. The only condition is your heartfelt belief in the Guide and your acceptance of His gift. You will have access to a Guidebook, which tells you all about the Guide and recounts stories of how others have journeyed with Him. The pamphlet does mention that others have agreed to take this journey, and you will be able to talk to them about their experiences with the Guide. At the end of the invitation, you notice an RSVP:

> Is anyone thirsty? Come and drink—even if you have no money! Come, take your choice of wine or milk—it's all free! Why spend your money on food that does not give you strength? Why pay for food that does you no good? Listen, and I will tell you where to get food that is good for the soul! Come to me with your ears wide open. Listen, for the life of your soul is at stake. I am ready to make an everlasting covenant with you. I will give you all the mercies and unfailing love that I promised to David. (Isa. 55:1–3 NLT)

High Noon
with Jesus

Her clothes seemed to smother her. It was so hot! Well, it should have been. It was high noon in the desert. And on the way back she would be carrying a full jar of water. She felt so weary.

But her fatigue was not just physical—her heart was tired. *Why am I such an outcast? I want someone to love . . . someone who will love me in return. I've tried! And the women . . . they won't even let me go to the well with them. . . . Wait, I see Someone at the well. What is a man doing here in this heat? Will He harm me? I've come this far. I'll get my water quickly and leave.*

"What? You want me, a Samaritan, to give You, a Jew, a drink? . . . Living water? Sounds like something I need. I want some! I hate coming to this well. . . . What? Call my husband? That's impossible; I don't have one. . . . Oh, uh, You must be a prophet. . . . Well, I'm not sure what You're saying about worship, but I know that the Messiah is coming!"

When some other men came to the well, she left. As she hurried back to the town, she thought, *What did He say? Yes, I heard Him. I know He said, "I am he. You don't have to wait any longer or look any further"* (John 4:26 *The Message*). She was breathless, and she no longer cared that people typically didn't listen to her. She shouted to all she saw, "Come see a man who knew all about the things I did, who knows me inside and out. Do you think this could be the Messiah?" (John 4:29 *The Message*).

The people from her town looked for Jesus, listened to Him, and then implored Him to stay with them. Afterward they said to the woman, "He's the Savior of the world!" (John 4:42 *The Message*).

"In what ways can you see yourself in the woman at the well?"

I love this story. I love Jesus for personally delivering His invitation to drink of His living water. I love Jesus for talking to this shunned woman at a well. Only Jesus would arrange a divine appointment with her.

In a sense we are all, in some way, outcasts until we meet the Lord. We are thirsty for people to love and accept us. We drink from many wells to try to satisfy our longings, but eventually, we tire of always having to draw water to get our needs met. Each of us asks, Isn't there someone who will give me water without manipulating me or requiring me to jump through hoops for it? Isn't there someone who will love me just for who I am?

Then Jesus appears at high noon. He tells us that He is the Son of God and that He wants to quench our thirst. He asks, "Do you need a Savior? Are you tired of looking for water for your soul? Do you believe that I died to redeem you from your sins and that you can have new life in Me?"

In a sense we are all, in some way, outcasts until we meet the Lord.

Why does He ask us to believe that He is the Savior of the world? Why is belief so essential to our journey to the heart of God? Because the woman at the well was a sinner, and so are we. I used to feel resentful about the fact that I seemed to be paying for what happened in the Garden of Eden. Then one day it dawned on me that if I had been in Eve's place, I would have responded just as she did; I would have desired fruit to make me wise. I am no different. I am a sinner, and sin has separated me from God. But God, in His love, bridges the gap with the Cross. If I am to journey toward the heart of a holy God, I must turn away from sin, receive forgiveness at the cross of Christ, and become a new creation.

Paul proclaimed in Romans 3:22–24,

> God's own way of giving men right standing with Himself is through faith in Jesus Christ. It is for everybody who has faith, for no distinction at all is made. For everybody has sinned and everybody continues to come short of God's glory, but anybody may have right standing with God as a free gift of His undeserved favor, through the ransom provided in Christ Jesus. (WILLIAMS)

What God's Invitation Cost Him

"The centre of salvation is the Cross of Jesus," wrote Oswald Chambers, "and the reason it is so easy to obtain salvation is because it cost God so much. The Cross is the point where God and sinful man merge with a crash and the way to life is opened—but the crash is on the heart of God."[2]

I have thought a lot about Jesus' death on the cross. I used to wonder why Jesus prayed in the garden to "let this cup [the Cross] pass from Me" (Matt. 26:39 NASB). It is common knowledge that thousands of people died by crucifixion; Jesus was not the only one who endured that cruel death. I concluded that it was not the physical agony He was asking to escape. It dawned on me that Jesus had never known sin. He had never been separated from His Father.

Then one day it dawned on me that if I had been in Eve's place, I would have responded just as she did.

The thought of becoming sin and of having His Father forsake Him grieved Him so deeply that His sweat became like drops of blood. Christ's plea, "Not My will, but Thine be done," revealed His longing to please His Father. But it also disclosed the depth of His love for us. How can we refuse such an incredible sacrifice—Christ's becoming sin for us—when the result is our cleansing, our right to become beloved children of God?

God's invitation is written with the blood of Jesus Christ. When we believe in and accept Christ's atoning sacrifice, we are brought into a relationship with our Father that enables us to journey toward His heart of love, forgiveness, reconciliation, and new birth. All God asks is that we admit our need for a Savior, turn away from the path of sin we have been on, and turn in faith to God with a desire to live for Him.

This belief is also an anchor to my faith. When I encounter hard times and I struggle with circumstances or relationships, I am reminded that because I believe, I have eternal life, I am God's own child, and I am loved by an everlasting love. God's question to me then becomes, *Aren't My love and the promise of eternal life enough to keep you on your journey? If nothing ever changes and you continue to go through difficulty, you will still have a lifetime of knowing Me and the blessing of living with Me forever.*

After the disciples returned from their first missionary journey and exclaimed to Jesus that even evil spirits submitted to their authority, Jesus redirected their enthusiasm. Instead of celebrating their power over demons, He said, they should rejoice that their names were recorded in the heavenly Book of Life. To know that my name is written in the Book of Life thrusts me on an incredible journey toward an entirely new life.

Just what are we asked to believe? The Creator of the universe—the holy, majestic, all-powerful, unconditionally loving, redeeming God—wants to adopt us. He wants us to live eternally with Him, to experience freedom from the power of sin, to know the joy of fellowship with Him and others, and to rely on His strength for continuing on our journey. The Cross secured this adoption. He waits for our response. He waits for us to knock at His gate.

―――

"Have you knocked at the gate of heaven,
admitting your need for a Savior?"

―――

Saying Yes to God

What was life like for the woman at the well after she believed Jesus?

I am loved. I am free. I am a new creation. My sins are forgiven. I am cleansed. It doesn't matter what others think—I have met the Messiah, and He has given me new life. I know that I am fully and completely loved. I have tasted the living water, and I no longer thirst.

I like to think that the man who was living with this woman at the time she met Jesus heard her testimony and believed. I like to think of him as one of the Samaritans who confirmed her experience with the proclamation, "He's the Savior of the world!" I like to imagine that they married, that she became transformed by Christ's love, and that others honored her because she was the chosen instrument of their Savior for the good news He preached. I like to picture her surrounded by women whenever she drew water from the well.

> **Aren't My love and the promise of eternal life enough to keep you on your journey?**

Her journey before she encountered Christ was one of despair, hurt, rejection. It was a journey bereft of hope. After her meeting with Christ, her belief propelled her onto a new path . . . a new journey . . . a new direction. She had left the City of Destruction and was on her way to Mount Zion. No more traveling through a series of damaging relationships. Her journey was now with her Lord, who would never leave her or forsake her. She would certainly experience pain again, but she would no longer bear it alone. Her destination was now the very heart of God.

"How would you describe your ultimate destination in life?"

Without belief, the "gate" cannot be opened so that we can begin our pilgrimage. Believing in Christ's sacrifice on the cross and our need for a Savior is indispensable to our journey.

"Repentance, the first word in Christian immigration," states Eugene Peterson, "sets us on the way to traveling in the light. It is a rejection that is also an acceptance, a leaving that develops into an arriving, a no to the world that is a yes to God."[3]

The year was 1951. It was Palm Sunday. I was twelve years old and standing at the front of the sanctuary of the church I attended. The pastor asked me, "Do you believe that Jesus Christ is the Son of God and that He died for your sins?"

"Yes, sir," I replied. That night, as a public testimony to my acceptance of Christ, I was baptized.

I had just said yes to God's RSVP.

Do you feel, with Christian, that you are a poor, burdened sinner coming from the City of Destruction with a desire to travel to Mount Zion? Perhaps you have not yet responded to God's invitation. If so, then a simple, heartfelt yes is all that is needed to open wide the gate. As you walk through, you will begin your pilgrimage to a heavenly destination.

And if you have responded to God's invitation, be refreshed with the assurance of God's great love for you and that you now live to journey to His heart.

> *I heard the voice of Jesus say,*
> *"Behold, I freely give*
> *The living water; thirsty one,*
> *Stoop down, and drink, and live."*
> *I came to Jesus, and I drank*
> *Of that life-giving stream;*
> *My thirst was quenched, my soul revived,*
> *And now I live in Him.* [4]

THREE

Relinquish Control

> Resolved, never, henceforward, till I die, to act as if I were any way my own, but entirely and altogether God's.
>
> Jonathan Edwards[1]

Going on a tour is very different from embarking on a solo personal vacation. When you sign up for a planned excursion, you accept the itinerary for that particular trip. You agree to whatever modes of transportation will be necessary. Once you are under way, you can't decide that you are free to eat at a different restaurant or stay at another hotel. You must also accept the accompaniment of the other people who have committed for the tour. The tour guide sets the schedule, and everyone in the group must comply.

I remember one occasion in which we were rushed from a historic landmark to visit what I felt was an obvious tourist trap. I was frustrated and felt that I should have been in control! The tour was not meeting *my* needs. By agreeing to go on the tour, however, I had relinquished my right to make such choices.

For many of us, one of the greatest challenges in our spiritual journey is letting go of our desire to exercise control.

*"Where in your life is it hardest for you
to give up control?"*

Portrait
of Surrender

She was packing for a journey from which she would not return. Her heart was heavy, for she was leaving her parents, her country, everything she knew. Her husband was buried here, and she would probably never see his grave again.

She was going with her mother-in-law to a foreign country. She *wanted* to go. After she had married into this family, she had discovered something wonderful, something spiritual. She had found God. Because her mother-in-law, Naomi, had lost her husband and two sons, Naomi longed to return to her own country. The famine there was over, and it was time for her to be with her people.

> *For many of us, one of the greatest challenges in our spiritual journey is letting go of our desire to exercise control.*

Strangely, Ruth felt that they were her people too. They were God's chosen, and she believed with them. Without Naomi, she would be left alone in her knowledge and worship of God. She needed to go with her mother-in-law, not only to be a good daughter-in-law, but most of all to grow in her understanding of God.

Naomi had made it very clear to her that going to Bethlehem meant a life of just the two of them living together. The conditions would be difficult for two widows. Ruth would be the one to glean in the fields for their food. Gleaning was a practice that allowed poor people to follow the reapers during the harvest and gather the grain that had been left behind. Not only would it be hard work, but it would subject her to ridicule and prejudice. It would make her vulnerable to the men who worked in the fields. But any sacrifice was worthy of this God she had found, and she was committed to seeking refuge under His wings, among His people.

Ruth willingly submitted to the process God had chosen for her on the journey toward His heart. Her willingness was exemplified by her commitment to move to Bethlehem and by her beautiful proclamation to Naomi, "I will go wherever you go and live wherever you live. Your people will be my people, and your God will be my God. I will die where you die and will be buried there" (Ruth 1:16–17 NLT).

Think of what Ruth was so gladly volunteering for: a trip to a strange country with a discouraged mother-in-law. There were no enticements, only the reality of the severity of life. Yet Ruth's "pull" to go on the journey was the heart of God, and if it meant relinquishing all she knew and held dear, so be it. She had counted the cost, and God was worthy of her life.

Choosing to Say No

"If anyone chooses to be my disciple," Jesus said, "he must say 'No' to self, put the cross on his shoulders daily, and continue to follow me" (Luke 9:23 WILLIAMS).

If I choose to believe God, then I must accept His plan and His route for my journey. The Moffatt translation of Hebrews 12:1 says that we must "run our appointed course." God has purchased us by sacrificing His Son, and we are now His children. He is our Father, and He lovingly takes responsibility for our lives. My part is to trust Him by giving up my agenda, saying no to self, and allowing Him to be in control.

This surrender is essential for our journey if we are to follow God's designated path for us. The way that we relinquish, give up, and yield to the Lord is to lay aside, strip off, and put to death the old self, so that we can put on the new self that we receive when we come to Christ.

═══════

*"Are you trusting God for the route
your journey may take?"*

═══════

Caught in the Act of Being Imperfect

The old self will pay any price to be loved and accepted. Consider the woman at the well, who was willing to be with anyone who might show her favor and approval. When we strive to get approval, when we maneuver people and circumstances for our benefit, we are saying a giant yes to the old self. Then when we don't receive the recognition we think we deserve, we blame ourselves or become bitter toward others.

I clipped a *Peanuts* cartoon by Charles Schulz in which Sally brings a sock to Charlie Brown. "Look," she says, "I'm missing a sock. . . . What can I do with one sock?" Charlie Brown replies, "Put it in your drawer until the second one shows up." Sally answers, "I tried that. The other socks wouldn't accept him!"

I felt like that lone sock one time when I was speaking at a church retreat. We were meeting in a hotel, and our first event together was dinner, after which I was scheduled to speak. I was unfamiliar with this part of the country, and I knew no one. Since the atmosphere at retreats is usually casual, I donned my favorite denim dress and found my way to the meeting room. When I opened the door, I saw lovely, beautifully dressed women sitting at lovely, beautifully decorated, candlelit tables. I gasped inwardly. My blue-jean dress seemed so out of place. *Oh, Lord,* I cried, *what will these women think of me? I'm not even dressed for the occasion! They won't like me! Why can't I at least look appropriate?*

I had no choice but to walk in and sit with my fear of not being accepted. While I was speaking after the meal, I mentioned my insecurity in not being dressed for the occasion. Following the meeting, a dear woman came up to me and said, "You know, I noticed that you had on a denim dress, but then I remembered that you're from the Southwest—and for you, that *is* being dressed up!" Perhaps a good antidote to insecurity is to live in the Southwest!

Later on, as I prayed over my feelings of inadequacy and near panic because I hadn't worn the right clothes, the Lord graciously reminded me of His love and acceptance. Then He brought to mind a conversation I'd had with Him. I had told Him that at my age, I would consider it a good day if I'm clothed and in my right mind! I laughed, but again I had to be reminded of the truth of His unconditional love. He looks at my heart. He accepts me in denim dresses. My journey is toward His heart, not toward acceptance from others. I dress and speak for Him.

One night we had company for dinner and I fixed baked chicken breasts. We said the blessing and began to eat. I was mortified at what happened next. As we cut into the chicken, blood trickled out. I could have died! *Here I am a grown woman and I still can't cook,* I thought to myself. *That's it—I'm never having people over again!* Yet another lesson in stripping off the old self.

The old self is always ready to rear its ugly head and tell me I need to be perfect. What is the truth? I will never be perfect while I'm on my journey. I love Peter for following Jesus through his own failures, and I love Paul for confessing that he was the chief of all sinners. God knows that we are always in process.

These experiences have helped me realize that what is important to God is the way I respond when I am confronted with my inadequacies. Do I condemn myself? Do I blame others? Do I get mad at God for creating me this way? Is my significance bound up in being perfect for everyone? When thoughts like these assail me, I go to the One who knows and accepts me just as I am. I ask for His truth to speak to my heart. He comforts me with the assurance that He has no expectations of flawlessness from me. And He helps me discern how to respond appropriately, in attitude or action, in front of those who witness my shortcomings.

We are continually being transformed and moving toward conformity to Christ. Now that I am in Christ, I can "lay aside" the self that demands perfection. I smiled when I saw this proclamation on a plaque: "I've given up my quest for perfection—I'm shooting for five good minutes!"

*"How do you respond when you are faced
with your own inadequacies or shortcomings?"*

The Temptation to Play It Safe

No woman likes to be vulnerable or to take risks that might reveal she is not perfect. Who wants to be placed in a position in which she will be rejected or experience pain? But seeking this protection from being hurt because we are not in control is part of the old self. God asks us to lay it aside.

Orpah, Ruth's sister-in-law, chose not to go with Naomi and Ruth to Naomi's homeland. One of the most lamentable scenes in Scripture occurred when Orpah kissed her mother-in-law good-bye, for in doing so she was turning away from the God of Israel. When Ruth insisted on staying with Naomi, her mother-in-law gave her one more chance to back out. "See," Naomi said to her, "your sister-in-law has gone back to her people and to her gods. You should do the same" (Ruth 1:15 NLT).

Ruth's "pull" to go on the journey was the heart of God, and if it meant relinquishing all she knew and held dear, so be it.

Orpah chose not to take the risk. She wanted to protect herself from the unknown and stay where it was safe and familiar. She chose allegiance to the gods of her country—the worship of Baal. She did not go on the journey to Bethlehem.

I grew up learning to shield myself from pain. The method of protection I developed was simply to tolerate hurtful relationships or circumstances through withdrawal and compromise. Consequently, I find it hard to put on the new self and speak the truth in love, especially when there might be a need to confront others.

The preacher Tony Evans provides a spiritual lesson in the analogy of owning versus renting a home. If you're the home owner and your roof needs replacing, who pays for the new roof? You do! But if you rent your home and it's time for a new roof, who pays? Not you, but the owner. And so it is spiritually. Who owns you? If you need repairing or protecting, who bears the expense: you or God?

If God "owns" me, then I don't have to protect myself. One of my favorite Scriptures is Psalm 27:1:

> The LORD is my light and my salvation;
> Whom shall I fear?

The LORD is the defense of my life;
Whom shall I dread? (NASB)

He is my protector, my shield, my defense. As I give my life to Him, it becomes His life. As my "home owner," He is in control. It is very freeing to rent!

———

"Is there an area of your life in which you
need to relinquish control to the Lord?"

———

"I Give Up!"

I will never forget the summer of 1965. We had just moved to Temple, Texas. I had three children under three years old. My husband was a very busy veterinarian with a large and small animal practice. Since Jack was rarely at home, it was a good thing that our house was situated right next to the animal clinic. We could go next door anytime we wanted to see what he looked like!

I felt as if I had been signed up for a crash course in flexibility. One of my first lessons was that cows who had difficulty calving had a sixth sense about when the doctor was sitting down to a meal with his family. Another was that my children and I were not the only beneficiaries of being housed next door to the clinic. The proximity was very convenient for local rodents, who could eat at the hospital and then come to our home to nest and play. One day it hit me that we were running a bed-and-breakfast for rats! I also picked up special skills in interior design. The house was an extremely old duplex—two front doors, two kitchens. As a family of five, we needed both sides, and so I learned how to decorate a kitchen as a bedroom.

My part is to trust Him by giving up my agenda, saying no to self, and allowing Him to be in control.

I spent that summer of '65 with wallpaper hanging down from the ceilings . . . rats running up and down the walls . . . cooking in a kitchen with one small sink flanked by a scant foot of counter space on either side . . . an absent husband . . . two babies in diapers and a newborn who wasn't sleeping . . . and no close friends. I was more than ready to sign up for a tour in which I didn't have to be in charge!

One afternoon I went to our room, stretched out across the bed, and cried out to God, "I give up!" I was so tired of trying to live life in my own strength. The Lord gently spoke these thoughts to my heart: *Good, Cynthia—I've been waiting for you to give up.*

In the quiet that followed, I remembered an illustration I'd heard a few months before. When we are born, we are given a car to drive down the highway of life. At twelve, I had stopped my car and invited Jesus Christ into my life. But then I put Him in the backseat and kept driving. Now, at twenty-six, I realized He was tapping me on the shoulder and asking me to move over. It was an opportunity to let Him take over the steering wheel of my life. I knew what He wanted, and I knew the cost involved. I would no longer be driving, so I would no longer be in control.

> *The old self is always ready to rear its ugly head and tell me I need to be perfect.*

I yielded that afternoon. I signed up for the whole tour. The itinerary was His; the lodging (definitely the lodging!) was His; my family, my routine, and my rats were all His. An amazing thing happened that day. Not one part of my life changed outwardly. In fact, we lived in that old house for four more years. I still had three small children who needed me constantly, and Jack was as busy as ever. But there was an *inward* change. I saw things differently. Relinquishment brought freedom, peace, the ability to persevere, and an inner joy. I no longer owned my life.

That summer I lost my life, and in the losing I found Life. Eugene Peterson's rendering of Luke 9:23–25 in *The Message* describes the reality I embraced:

> Anyone who intends to come with me has to let me lead. You're not in the driver's seat—I am. Don't run from suffering; embrace it. Follow me and I'll show you how. Self-help is no help at all. Self-sacrifice is the way, *my* way, to finding yourself, your true self. What good would it do to get everything you want and lose you, the real you?

My experience was one of first accepting Christ as Savior and then later realizing that He was also Lord of my life and worthy of being in control. Christ cannot be divided. He is both Savior and Lord. But sometimes our response to His lordship varies. I think that when Ruth first believed God, she also embraced Him as her Lord, all at the same time. What is important is that we understand He is our Savior and our Lord. As we embrace Him in His fullness, He sets us on a firm foundation for our journey.

✿✿

"Anyone who might feel reluctant to surrender his will to the will of another," observed A. W. Tozer, "should remember Jesus' words, 'Whosoever committeth sin is the servant of sin' (John 8:34). We must of necessity be servant to someone, either to God or to sin."[2]

When we choose to stay in control, we are in effect choosing to be controlled by someone or something other than God. Orpah thought she was maintaining control by choosing to reject the unknown and stay behind in the country that was familiar to her. She "saved" her life by spending the rest of it in Moab, worshiping Baal. Ruth relinquished control by leaving behind the life she had known and choosing to trust God. In that "losing," she met and married Boaz, became the great-grandmother of King David, and acquired lasting recognition as one of five women cited in the lineage of Christ.

> *Seeking protection from being hurt because we are not in control is part of the old self. God asks us to lay it aside.*

The outcome of your journey depends on your decision. If you live your life forever calculating relationships and staying on your guard, you will be forever burdened with *self*, and you will arrive at the end of your journey weary and disappointed. Although it seems safe and logical to be in charge of your life, being in charge becomes a heavy, lonely responsibility. Your Father graciously offers to take your life, protect you, strengthen you, and comfort you on your journey. You need not fear relinquishment, for it leads to freedom, security, and the real you.

All to Jesus I surrender,
All to Him I freely give;
I will ever love and trust Him,
In His presence daily live.[3]

Faith for the Unforeseen

Fragile trust is stronger than swaggering self-reliance.

Calvin Miller[1]

L oud shouts and screams interrupted our lunch. We had been touring the national parliament building in a foreign country, and we had seen demonstrators picketing the entrance on our way in. Now, midway through our meal in the cafeteria, we were startled by the rush of guards to lock all the doors. Just outside the windows, we could see an angry mob attacking, trying to shove their way into the building.

Our visit coincided with pending legislation that would affect the unions. The next day a crucial bill was to be passed, and the laborers were out to protest in force. Jack and I, along with our small group of tourists and the staff of government workers, were locked inside for the next three hours while police and rioters battled outside. There were casualties on both sides, and the new gift shop was plundered. During a lull in the violence, we were whisked out of the building through a back passageway usually reserved for official use.

Our experience that day underscored for me that when you're on a tour, you need to be prepared for the unexpected!

How freeing it is to recognize that when we are faced with danger or uncertainty, we do not have to panic. We can depend on God to control the outcome. Proverbs 3:5–6 has taught me to trust God no matter what circumstances I face: "Lean on, trust in, and be confident in the Lord with all your heart and mind and do not rely on your own insight or under-standing. In all your ways know, recognize, and acknowledge Him, and He will direct and make straight and plain your paths" (AMPLIFIED). That was a crucial issue for the Israelites, especially during their wilderness experience.

Danger Ahead

A crowd of Hebrews clustered around the leaders to hear their promo-tional pitch about a country that supposedly had everything they could want. The spokesmen for the tour told the group that the land had been specially chosen for its abundance of food (plenty of milk and honey) and spacious room for everyone to live.

The would-be tour guides promoting the journey were up front about the costs involved. There would certainly be skirmishes as they moved into the territory, but they guaranteed the people would be fully protected and victorious over all the inhabitants. The leaders' travel company had a long history and was very reliable. Although the journey would not be trouble-free, they could testify that it was absolutely the best tour any-one could take. They would miss the trip of a lifetime if they didn't go.

There were conflicting reports about the land, however. Some of the men who had been sent ahead on the scouting expedition had their own opinions about the risks involved. They reported that the land certainly did have large, lovely fruit. In fact, they had brought back a very large cluster of the season's first grapes hanging on display from a pole, along with some pomegranates and figs. The potential travelers could see for themselves that the food promised to be very good. But some of the

They had no faith for the unforeseen, no trust in the One who wanted them to go forward.

scouts were nevertheless discouraging the people from taking the jour-ney. Sure, the provisions would be first-rate, but they had no chance against the land's fierce inhabitants. They spread bad press everywhere. "We will be devoured!" they warned. "The men are huge, like giants, and we are like grasshoppers."

The people decided to focus on the potential risks instead of the promised blessings. In fact, they protested bitterly to their leaders for asking them to consider such a trip. Even slavery under their former oppressors would be better than taking such a risk! So instead of moving to a land flowing with milk and honey, the people chose to continue living as wanderers in the wilderness.

Why? They had no faith for the unforeseen, no trust in the One who wanted them to go forward.

Every time I read this story in the Scriptures, I want to shout to the Israelites, "Listen to Joshua and Caleb! Believe God! When He says He will be with you, He means it. When He has a plan for you, trust in His love, goodness, and provision. 'Fear not' is one of His favorite sayings. He goes before you in the battles you will face. If you only knew what He has planned for Jericho. You are going to miss out. Go! Listen to those who have faith. Giants are nothing to God, especially when He has promised victory. Go on the journey God has for you; the alternative is dying in the wilderness."

My shouting would be to no avail, for the Israelites were stubbornly set on their decision. I am always challenged by this passage of Scripture because it is such a graphic reminder of my need to trust God and the path He has for me, despite my dislike for giants and riots in foreign countries.

———

*"What giants do you fear in the land
where God is leading you?"*

———

Looks Can Be Deceiving

Paul declared that we walk by faith, not by sight (2 Cor. 5:7). This passage came to mind while I was reading in the Old Testament about the arguments between the herdsmen of Abram and Lot over pastureland. Abram approached Lot and made this offer, "We need to separate. Please, take your choice of any of the land you want." The Scriptures record Lot's decision: "Lot took a long look at the fertile plains of the Jordan Valley in the direction of Zoar. The whole area was well watered everywhere,

To walk by faith is to allow the Lord to choose the way for us, and then to trust Him with whatever lies ahead.

like the garden of the LORD or the beautiful land of Egypt" (Gen. 13:10 NLT).

What struck me about this verse is how easily we can be deceived by appearances. What really *looked good* to Lot from a distance was full of wickedness and perversion. He walked by sight and spent a lifetime weary of the immorality around him. The Israelites were also deceived by appearances. Although in reality Canaan was a promised land of peace and abundance, going there *looked bad* to them. They walked by sight and spent a lifetime camping and eating manna.

To walk by sight is to focus on overpowering hurdles and turn away from a God-directed path. It is to choose a path simply because it seems good and smooth, and then to realize it was the wrong choice. To walk by faith is to allow the Lord to choose the way for us, and then to trust Him with whatever lies ahead.

Oswald Chambers provided a helpful insight for choosing to walk by faith rather than sight:

> God sometimes allows you to get into a place of testing where your own welfare would be the right and proper thing to consider if you were not living a life of faith; but if you are, you will joyfully waive your right and leave God to choose for you. . . . It would seem the wisest thing in the world for Abraham to choose, it was his right, and the people around would consider him a fool for not choosing. Many of us do not go on spiritually because we prefer to choose what is right instead of relying on God to choose for us.[2]

Patience with the Unexpected

Giving up our right to be right is extremely difficult. It's hard to trust when what we see is so clear. It seems blatantly obvious to anyone with common sense. "Why do I have to let God choose? Doesn't He trust me?

Besides, I've tried to give God an opportunity to choose for me, but He never seems to be in a hurry. He is not on my timetable. I need to know immediately, but so often it seems as if He doesn't respond. Sure, I'm willing to have faith for the unexpected, but the hard part is when I do trust, God doesn't seem to move. I'm stuck at a crossroad, waiting for direction, and I wait and wait."

Giving up our right to be right is extremely difficult. It's hard to trust when what we see is so clear.

It seemed right to Sarai to help God out with His purpose by giving her maid, Hagar, to Abram. How else were they going to produce an heir—hadn't they waited ten years? Enough was enough. Time was wasting. God had promised a child, and she was only expediting His plan. Right? (I'm with you, Sarai; I don't even like red lights.)

It seemed right to Rebekah to intervene when Isaac was going to bless Esau. God had told her that Jacob was to have the blessing. "Hurry, Jacob, let's deceive your father. I need to help God out here. God is about to allow your father to do something He doesn't want him to do. This is unexpected! God is caught off guard. It's okay to be deceitful and to manipulate circumstances because we're helping to ensure that God's will is accomplished. We don't have time to wait. We have to take this into our own hands."

It seemed right to Martha and Mary that Jesus would arrive in time to heal their brother, Lazarus, who was gravely ill. They sent for Jesus with the message, "The one You love is very sick." And then they waited. The Lord would come. He dearly loved them all. He had healed so many; certainly, He would come quickly to this beloved family. They waited some more. Then Lazarus died.

Lazarus dead—it cannot be! Where on earth was Jesus? We had faith; He's the Messiah. He heals people. He responds to those He loves, and to those who love Him. His late arrival was totally unexpected.

When Jesus showed up after the fact, Martha told Him bluntly that He was too late. Jesus responded that *He* was the resurrection and the life. He taught her in a miraculous way that day to walk by faith instead of by sight.

═══

*"Are you struggling with walking by
faith instead of by sight?"*

═══

The journey to the heart of God is full of the difficult, the unexplained, and the unexpected. The reason is that it is God's journey. His thoughts and ways are not like our thoughts and ways. We're on our way to a heavenly home, and things are done differently in His kingdom. We have turned from the dominion of Satan to the kingdom of God. We get a taste here of this journey into His kingdom, and it's foreign to us. The teachings are new to us: love those who hate you . . . do good to those who despitefully use you . . . forgive over and over again . . . walk by faith, not by sight . . . wait. All kingdom teaching is contrary to the way the world instructs us to live.

People who have chosen to abide by the world's way of living must still deal with the unexpected, the unexplained, and the difficult. The difference for us is that God gives strength and grace, and He has an amazing ability to weave together all that happens to us for our good. Walking by faith provides hope and directs our lives toward all that is eternal.

We're on our way to a heavenly home, and things are done differently in His kingdom.

If we choose to be impatient with the unexpected and refuse to wait in trust for God's timing, then we have to live with the consequences.

If we are like Sarai, we have to live with an Ishmael—the son of her handmaid, who became a rival to her and Abram's son. From day one of her decision to interfere, trouble and antagonism ensued. She could have avoided all that by trusting in the timing of the Lord God.

If we are like Rebekah, we must live with the loss of a beloved child's presence. She succeeded in helping Jacob acquire his father's blessing, but she lost her son in the process. He also had to struggle with the repercussions of his deception. What did God want of Rebekah? Her fragile trust that He was able to fulfill His promise and arrange for Isaac to bless Jacob.

The experience of Martha and Mary encourages us to trust in the Lord's higher purposes, even in the face of great tragedy when nothing seems to make any sense. Sometimes we are privileged to see Him use and redeem our affliction. But when we don't see the visible results, we may safely trust that He always responds at the right time and in the right way, for His glory.

Choosing to Trust God

One of my more memorable travel experiences was circling Philadelphia in the midst of a storm. We flew over that brotherly city for quite a while. About every ten minutes, the pilot would update us: "Ladies and gentlemen, we still do not have clearance to land. We'll keep circling, and whenever I get any news, I'll let you know."

Each time the pilot told us that, the man sitting to my left became increasingly agitated and vented his anger. "I'm going to be caught right in the middle of rush-hour traffic!" he exclaimed. "There's no way I'm going to be on time for my appointment! I'm never flying this airline again!"

As we continued to go around and around, another man, sitting across the aisle from me to my right, became increasingly sick.

As I sat there between the two men, I began thinking, *I certainly don't like circling Philadelphia. In fact, I don't like circling any city! But apparently, this is part of the journey God has planned for me. There's nothing I can do about these circumstances, but I can choose how to respond to them.* One option would be to get angry. *Why did You put me here, God? I'm on a schedule too. This is really going to complicate matters.* I also thought of how easy it would be to grow anxious. *How much longer is this going to continue? What if the plane runs out of fuel? How am I going to work out all the details of rearranging plans for this evening?* And, of course, I could have responded by getting sick—or at least indulging in misery. I chose to accept God's change in plans. *Lord, I trust You for where I am right now. I want to receive Your grace and rest in what You have in store for me—however unexpected.*

——

*"In what respect would you like to deepen your patience
in waiting on God's plans?"*

——

Henri Nouwen pointed out that trusting God is an active choice, not a passive withdrawal from the pain and difficulty of life:

> As long as we have only a vague inner feeling of discontent with our present way of living, and only an indefinite desire for "things spiritual," our lives will continue to stagnate in a generalized melancholy. We often say, "I am not very happy. I am not content with the way my life is going. I am not really joyful or peaceful, but I just don't know how things can be different, and I guess I have to be realistic and accept my life as it is." It is this mood of resignation that prevents us from actively searching for the life of the Spirit.[3]

Stepping Out in Faith

It is easy to fear the unexpected, just as the Israelites did. Turn to the Scriptures, which God has given to guide and teach you. Learn from the lives of Lot, Sarai, and Rebekah—they will show you that if you rely on your insight, you will live with the consequences of choosing to do your own thing. According to Proverbs 16:25, "There is a path before each person that seems right, but it ends in death" (NLT). There is a high cost to living by the creed "I did it my way."

Trusting God—and allowing Him to choose for you—is the best assurance you can have for shouting down the walls of Jericho and conquering your fear of giants. Your journey will become exciting as you see God orchestrate the unforeseen for your good. This does not mean you will always find it a simple matter to discern God's leading and step out in faith. F. B. Meyer offered sound advice for how to rely on God's leading in daily choices:

> Beloved, whenever you are doubtful as to your course, submit your judgment absolutely to the Spirit of God, and ask Him to

shut against you every door but the right one. Say, "Blessed Spirit, I cast on Thee the entire responsibility of closing against my steps any and every course which is not of God. Let me hear Thy voice behind me whenever I turn to the right hand or the left." In the meanwhile, continue along the path which you have been already treading. Abide in the calling in which you are Called, unless you are clearly told to do something else. The Spirit of Jesus waits to be to you, O pilgrim, what He was to Paul. Only be careful to obey His least prohibition; and where after believing prayer, there are no apparent hindrances, go forward with enlarged heart.[4]

Will I visit other parliaments in foreign countries? Will I ever fly to Philadelphia again? Absolutely. Placing my faith in God for the unexpected keeps me from swaggering self-reliance.

> *Simply trusting every day,*
> *Trusting through a stormy way;*
> *Even when my faith is small,*
> *Trusting Jesus—that is all.*[5]

FIVE

Travel Light

Not many of us are living at our best. We linger in the lowlands because we are afraid to climb the mountains. The steepness and ruggedness dismay us, and so we stay in the misty valleys and do not learn the mystery of the hills. We do not know what we lose in our self-indulgence, what glory awaits us if only we had courage for the mountain climb, what blessing we should find if only we would move to the uplands of God.

J. R. M.[1]

One year my mother invited me to travel with her. One of the benefits of a directed tour is the luxury of allowing someone else to make sure your bags accompany you from one location to another. On the tour, most of the time we were responsible only to carry our bags from the hall into our rooms. It was a great arrangement, for we both had large suitcases plus our smaller carry-on bags. There were times, however, when we had to carry our luggage quite a distance to and from the tour bus and our rooms. Sometimes that involved stairs or elevators, which were rarely located anywhere close to our rooms. I remember one evening, after an exhausting day of travel and sight-seeing, arriving late at the next hotel. No one was there to help us carry our bags. I didn't want my mom to have to carry anything, so I had to make three trips up a long flight of stairs to get all our luggage to the room. In situations like that, we both wished we had traveled with lighter and fewer suitcases. The experience prompted me to purchase "lite" luggage. It also convinced me to pack wisely and take only the necessities.

To be unencumbered when we travel makes for a more enjoyable trip. To live in an uncluttered home makes it a place of rest, allowing us to give our time to what is most important. The same is true in our spiritual lives: the practice of laying aside unnecessary baggage will enable us to love and relate and serve with greater freedom and joy. To travel light spiritually is a gift we can give ourselves to make our journey the best it can be.

The Scriptures sometimes portray our pilgrimage as a race: "Let us strip off every weight that slows us down, especially the sin that so easily hinders our progress. And let us run with endurance the race that God has set before us" (Heb. 12:1 NLT).

Since each day is part of our journey, we are instructed to "strip down," "cast off," and "lay aside" any extra baggage that we might be lugging around with us. Have you ever seen marathon runners carrying weights as they compete? Runners wear only light clothing and shoes to enable them to endure a long race. And so our God urges us to travel *lightly* as we move toward His heart.

Laying Down Our Emotional Burdens

Perhaps you are all too aware of the kinds of things that weigh you down day to day. But what is most likely to make you spiritually tired? Listen to the psalmist David:

> When I kept silent about my sin, my body wasted away
> Through my groaning all day long.
> For day and night Thy hand was heavy upon me;
> My vitality was drained away as with the fever heat of summer.
> I acknowledged my sin to Thee,
> And my iniquity I did not hide;
> I said, "I will confess my transgressions to the LORD";
> And Thou didst forgive the guilt of my sin. (Ps. 32:3–5 NASB)

One of my constant prayers is, "Please, Lord, let me know when I sin." I can't imagine anything worse than hurting a friend or sinning against someone without being aware of it. David's image for this kind of knowing is, "Thy hand was heavy upon me." I love God for His desire that we become aware of our sin—not so that we wallow in shame, but so that we may confess our sin and be released from its weight, whatever that sin might be.

John gave us a wonderful assurance of this release in his first epistle: "If we say we have no sin, we are only fooling ourselves and refusing to accept the truth. But if we confess our sins to him, he is faithful and just to forgive us and to cleanse us from every wrong" (1 John 1:8–9 NLT). For example, when I become irritable with Jack, I will sometimes be curt and cool to him, putting an emotional distance between the two of us. Faithfully, the Holy Spirit will prompt me to confess my sin and be reconciled to my husband. Sometimes I struggle with this—but each time I obey, the heaviness lifts. I know once again that I have laid aside a burden, and closeness with Jack returns.

Through Christ's atoning death, these wonderful gifts become truly ours: forgiveness, release from guilt, freedom from the weight of sin, and thorough cleansing. Because we are forgiven, we are asked to extend the same gifts to others—and empowered to do so.

"Are you carrying a burden of sin
that you can lay aside in confession to God?"

The Burden
of Holding on
to Hurts

It isn't fair! I carried out my duty. I brought an offering. Why wasn't it accepted?
Why is it that my brother always seems to do the right thing, and somehow I
end up being in the wrong? God must like him better. As long as he's around,
I'm never going to measure up in God's eyes. Well, I'm just not going to put up

with this. My brother makes me sick. I can't stand the sight of him any longer. He's a pretentious do-gooder. He doesn't deserve to live.

God's response to Cain's embitterment was, "Why are you so angry? . . . Why do you look so dejected? You will be accepted if you respond in the right way. But if you refuse to respond correctly, then watch out! Sin is waiting to attack and destroy you, and you must subdue it" (Gen. 4:6–7 NLT).

Here is one of many examples in the Bible of how unresolved anger turns to bitterness. Bitterness will literally attack and destroy us. One of its destructive consequences is that we acquire a heavy burden. The longer we hold on to it, the heavier this burden tends to become—and the harder it is to discard. Bitterness has a particular tendency to settle in and take root in our lives. Because of this, God gives us specific instruction regarding how to handle our anger: "And 'don't sin by letting anger gain control over you.' Don't let the sun go down while you are still angry, for anger gives a mighty foothold to the Devil" (Eph. 4:26–27 NLT).

Whether anger is justified or unjustified, we must respond to it correctly and bring it under control. If we do not, we give the devil a prime opportunity to do damage. It's interesting that God told Cain, "Sin is waiting to attack and destroy *you*." Anger not only destroys others; it destroys us too. The admonition is not to let the anger take control. Instead, we must acknowledge it and handle it appropriately by confronting it quickly.

I love the Psalms for the honesty with which they voice human emotion, and their wisdom in demonstrating by example how we can deal with anger and hurt. Psalms 55 and 109, for example, illuminate specific ways in which David gained control over some very intense emotions. David had been devastated by the discovery that his companion and close friend had suddenly become his enemy.

Here are some of David's thoughts concerning the betrayal of his former friend:

> Arrange for an evil person to turn on him. . . .
> Count his prayers as sins.
> Let his years be few. . . .
> Let no one be kind to him. . . .
> May all his offspring die. . . .

May his mother's sins never be erased from the record.
    (Ps. 109:6, 7, 8, 12, 13, 14 NLT)

Now listen to David's prayer in the wake of acknowledging his agonizing betrayal:

> But I will call on God,
>   and the LORD will rescue me.
> Morning, noon, and night
>   I plead aloud in my distress,
>   and the LORD hears my voice.
> He rescues me and keeps me safe
>   from the battle waged against me,
>   even though many still oppose me. (Ps. 55:16–18 NLT)

There's no mistaking that David was angry! He was ruthlessly honest in declaring exactly how he thought God should deal with his betrayer. David's thoughts toward the man were not kind. But David was right to vent his feelings in prayer to God, for only as we acknowledge our anger before God are we able to respond appropriately.

It amazes me that the Lord truly wants us to come to Him with even our most harsh thoughts. I used to think that if I didn't tell God, I could somehow keep Him from knowing my true feelings! But David called to God morning, noon, and night. I think that every time David felt pain over that rejection, he complained and murmured about it to God. Over and over again, saying the very same thing, David expressed his anger and hurt. Here is an antidote to bitterness. And here is a way to grieve a loss. Morning, noon, and evening—for days, weeks, and perhaps months—David released his feelings by crying out to the Lord.

———

"What feelings would you like to release by
crying out to the Lord?"

———

David learned firsthand the wisdom that he passed along to us:

> Give your burdens to the LORD,
>   and he will take care of you.
>   He will not permit the godly to slip and fall. (Ps. 55:22 NLT)

In casting our burdens upon the Lord, we relieve ourselves of the weight of trying to set things right. We can rest in the knowledge that God will deal justly with wrongdoing. Because He rescues us and keeps us safe from destruction, we can be set free from the impulse to take revenge:

> Dear friends, never avenge yourselves. Leave that to God. For it
> is written,
> > "I will take vengeance;
> > > I will repay those who deserve it,"
> > says the Lord. (Rom. 12:19 NLT)

Keeping
Short Accounts

As we journey to the heart of God, we must remember that His commands are like signposts along the way—they have been placed there for our good to keep us traveling safely in the right direction. Since He created us, He knows what is best for us—and therefore we must be alert and obedient to His words.

God wants us to control our anger and deal with it quickly, for it has a unique and deadly potential to weigh us down. He instructs us to keep short accounts with Him: *confess your sin and be cleansed.* As we seek forgiveness for ourselves, we are also commanded to forgive others. I don't think we need to sit around and debate the meaning of the following verses:

> And forgive us our sins,
> > just as we have forgiven those who have sinned against us.
> (Matt. 6:12 NLT)

> If you forgive those who sin against you, your heavenly Father will
> forgive you. But if you refuse to forgive others, your Father will
> not forgive your sins. (Matt. 6:14–15 NLT)

Forgiving others is one of God's foremost commands of us. It is so imperative that God explains the alarming repercussions of our failure to forgive: *we* will not receive forgiveness! Lawrence Richards provides a helpful explanation of this hard truth: "It isn't that God will not forgive the unforgiving. It is simply that the unforgiving lack the humble attitude that both permits them to accept forgiveness and frees them to extend forgiveness."2

Forgiveness is essential to our welfare. In fact, forgiving others is more important for our benefit than for the one who has wounded us because it frees us from the offender's hold over us, and it removes any barrier to receiving the forgiveness of God in our lives.

*"What are your greatest needs for giving
and receiving forgiveness?"*

His own brothers wanted to kill him. They couldn't agree on just how that should be done, so they decided to sit down over a meal and work out the details. While they were dining, one family member proposed that they sell the unwanted brother to a traveling caravan as a slave. So much for brotherly love.

I have often thought about the extraordinary pain Joseph must have endured. To be hated and rejected by your family is to be left feeling totally forsaken and alone. As Joseph became a slave and then a prison inmate, he could have allowed his anger to turn into deep bitterness. Forgiveness might well have been the farthest thought from his mind. *"Forgive?* Those who so brutally spurned me? Absolutely not! It's not right, and it's not fair. I'm the one who has had to suffer. I'm the one who has paid all these years for their sin. If I ever see them again, *I'll* make *them* pay."

But Joseph chose a different path of response to the unforeseen affliction in his life. He refused to let a weight of bitterness drag him down. Listen to the words he spoke to his brothers when they became fearful of what he might do to them now that he had risen to power as the prime minister of Egypt:

> But Joseph told them, "Don't be afraid of me. Am I God, to judge
> and punish you? As far as I am concerned, God turned into good
> what you meant for evil. He brought me to the high position I
> have today so I could save the lives of many people. No, don't be
> afraid. Indeed, I myself will take care of you and your families."

And he spoke very kindly to them, reassuring them. (Gen. 50:19–21 NLT)

Rather than become embittered and seek revenge, Joseph walked by faith when he encountered heartache and false accusations. He trusted God with his past, his present, and his future. In faith, he believed that God was *for* him. God was at work to turn all those "detours" into paths leading to Joseph's ultimate good. And so Joseph relinquished control. He forgave.

A burden is anything in our lives that hinders our journey toward God. Unnecessary weights slow us down, make us tired, and keep us from persevering. We begin to focus on our burdens, and in consequence we eventually turn our eyes away from the Lord. We all pick up unnecessary weights in the course of our journey, which we must continually lay aside throughout our lives. The heaviest ones entail confessing sin, dealing with anger, and choosing to forgive. Others ease themselves more subtly into our carry-on bags—the love of money, the legacy of the past, fear, the world, anxiety. We need to maintain a vigilant scrutiny of what we are stuffing into our backpacks.

We linger in the lowlands because carrying a heavy load to the mountains is too exhausting. What blessing and glory await us as we move in freedom to the uplands of God! We have a choice. Ultimately, each of us must ask, How do I want to journey in this life—plodding along, weighed down with heavy burdens? Or running the race in the freedom of confession, self-control, and forgiveness? Where do I want to spend my life—in the misty valleys or the mysterious hills? Since we carry our own bags on this excursion of life, why not choose to travel light?

"What changes can you make to travel light in your journey with God?"

The Freedom of Inner Healing

Corrie Ten Boom, the precious saint who endured cruel and inhuman treatment in a German concentration camp, had just spoken at a church in Munich. Afterward, she was stunned to see one of her former captors approaching her. Her heart stood still as he came up to her, extended his hand, and introduced himself as one of the guards at Ravensbruck.

Since the war he had become a Christian, he said. "I know that God has forgiven me for the cruel things I did there," he confessed, "but I would like to hear it from your lips as well." Then, his hand outstretched, he asked her directly, "Will you forgive me?"

Corrie described the thoughts that raced through her mind at that moment:

> And I stood there—I whose sins had every day to be forgiven—
> and could not. Betsie had died in that place—could he erase her
> slow terrible death simply for the asking?
>
> It could not have been many seconds that he stood there, hand
> held out, but to me it seemed hours as I wrestled with the most
> difficult thing I had ever had to do.
>
> For I had to do it—I knew that. The message that God forgives
> has a prior condition: that we forgive those who have injured us.
> "If you do not forgive men their trespasses," Jesus says, "neither
> will your Father in heaven forgive your trespasses." I knew it not
> only as a commandment of God, but as a daily experience.

Corrie had opened a home in Holland for people who had suffered terribly at the hands of the Nazi regime. She knew that those who were able to forgive their former enemies were most likely to find their way back to rebuilt lives. Those who held on to their bitterness remained crippled by it. Yet still she felt powerless to respond:

> I stood there with the coldness clutching my heart. But forgiveness
> is not an emotion—I knew that too. Forgiveness is an act of the
> will, and the will can function regardless of the temperature of the
> heart. "Jesus, help me!" I prayed silently. "I can lift my hand. I can
> do that much. You supply the feeling."
>
> And so woodenly, mechanically, I thrust my hand into the one
> stretched out to me. And as I did, an incredible thing took place.
> The current started in my shoulder, raced down my arm, sprang
> into our joined hands. And then the healing warmth seemed to
> flood my whole being, bringing tears to my eyes.

"I forgive you, brother!" I cried. "With all my heart!"

For a long moment we grasped each other's hands, the former guard and the former prisoner. I had never known God's love so intensely as I did then.[3]

Not all experiences of forgiveness happen in a single moment, however. The Lord is gracious to deal with each of us according to our individual needs, especially in our places of deepest struggle and hurt. Brennan Manning points out that it may take time to experience God's release from our inner burdens:

> Experientially, the inner healing of the heart is seldom a sudden catharsis or an instant liberation from bitterness, anger, resentment, and hatred. More often it is a gentle growing into oneness with the Crucified who has achieved our peace through His blood on the cross. This may take considerable time because the memories are still so vivid and the hurt is still so deep. But it *will* happen. The crucified Christ is not merely heroic example to the church: He is the power and wisdom of God, a living force in His present risenness, transforming our lives and enabling us to extend the hand of reconciliation to our enemies.[4]

Perhaps you realize that you are carrying excess baggage on your journey. The weight of past hurts, anger, and bitterness has settled in, and you are weary. God desires to grant forgiveness and to see you walk in newness and freedom. He wants you to share with Him all of your feelings so that you can experience release. Pray to the Lord now, cast your burden upon Him, and then leave it there. Ask for the necessary grace to forgive others. Allow the Lord to gently grow you into oneness with Him, and then race to the mountains.

Are we weak and heavy laden,
Cumbered with a load of care?
Precious Savior, still our refuge
Take it to the Lord in prayer![5]

Fellowship with Our Guide

Being led by someone assumes a continuing relationship. It implies fellowship. It brings to mind cooperation, sensitivity, and common goals. When someone is following another, there must be trust, even to the point of dependency. All of these describe the believer's relationship with the Holy Spirit as the person allows Him to be the guide.

Charles Stanley[1]

O f the tour guides I have met, most were pleasant, capable individuals who were concerned for the group as a whole. However, a couple of them did not seem to have the time or inclination to get to know everyone personally on the tour. I formed no lasting friendships with them, and now I have even forgotten their names.

Unlike most tour guides, our Guide to the heart of God wants to be at the very center of our journey, closely joined to us. He is a wonderful Teacher, but He does far more than provide instruction. He walks with us every step of the way, offering His constant presence as a personal and intimate companion. When we grow tired, He helps us to lay down our burdens, and He refreshes us. When we are lonely, He reminds us that He has never left our side. He promises that He will never fail or forsake us. Always, He invites us to draw closer to Him.

Hear the voice of our Lord: "Come to me, all of you who are weary and carry heavy burdens, and I will give you rest. Take my yoke upon you. Let me teach you, because I am humble and gentle, and you will find rest for your souls. For my yoke fits perfectly, and the burden I give you is light" (Matt. 11:28–30 NLT).

At the Feet of Jesus

Jesus was in their home! Oh, how she longed to be with Him. Nothing mattered—preparing the food, setting the table, refilling the water glasses. All she wanted was to sit at His feet, to listen to His words. Compared to the richness of this time, everything else faded into obscurity. He was her Lord. He wanted to teach her, refresh her, and enjoy her company. She couldn't imagine being anywhere else.

Mary of Bethany wanted to be where Jesus was. Remaining with Him took priority over serving. When her sister, Martha, questioned Jesus about Mary's choice not to help her in the kitchen, Jesus lovingly rebuked Martha—not for her service, but for her worry and preoccupation that kept her from the one thing for which she should have been concerned.

That doesn't mean we're supposed to be part Mary and part Martha. Jesus didn't say, "Oh, Martha, you're right. Now, Mary, you've been sitting here long enough; you go into the kitchen. Martha, it's your turn to sit down." Jesus clearly said, "There is really only one thing worth being concerned about. Mary has discovered it—and I won't take it away from her" (Luke 10:42 NLT).

The one thing Mary had discovered was the joy of abiding. To abide is to stay, to continue, to remain. A house is an abode. If we abide with someone, it's as if we are living with that person in the same house. Mary was, in effect, "staying" with Jesus.

My definition of *abiding* is "consistently sitting at the feet of Jesus and continually depending upon Him by listening to His words with a heart to obey." J. Oswald Sanders wrote, "It means keeping unbroken contact with Christ in a union of intimate love."[2]

"Have you tasted the joy of abiding?"

At this point you may be thinking, *If abiding is the one thing worth being concerned about, how do I do it? There are so many legitimate distractions on this journey, I can't always be sitting at the feet of Jesus. In fact, when does anyone find time just to sit?*

The most helpful response I can give you is, "Don't think of Jesus' call to come to Him as yet another activity you must schedule into your day." When Jesus came to her home, Mary of Bethany didn't say with a sigh, "Oh, no, here's Jesus. Now I have to spend time with Him." The call is to come and be yoked to Him—to walk with Him, to remain with Him, and to commune with Him throughout the day. Since He is always with us, our abiding is continual.

> *This time with God doesn't require much of us—just quieting ourselves before Him, conversing with Him about what is on our hearts, and being simple and honest.*

David Brainerd, a missionary in the early eighteenth century, recorded this entry in his journal: "In the morning I was very busy in preparation for my journey, and was almost continually engaged in ejaculatory prayer."[3] Although his activities were driven by a crowded list of tasks, the whole time he was talking with the Lord.

Brother Lawrence, a seventeenth-century Christian, learned the practice of abiding in the midst of his daily work in a monastery kitchen:

> I renounced for the love of Him, everything that was not He, and
> I began to live as if there was none but He and I in the world. . . .
> But when we are faithful to keep ourselves in His holy presence,
> and set Him always before us, this not only hinders our offending
> Him and doing anything that may displease Him, at least willfully,
> but it also begets in us a holy freedom, and, if I may so speak, a
> familiarity with God, wherewith we ask and, that successfully, the

graces we stand in need of. . . . I cannot imagine how religious persons can live satisfied without the *practice of the presence of God*. For my part, I keep myself retired with Him in the fund or center of my soul as much as I can; and while I am so with Him I fear nothing, but the least turning from Him is insupportable.[4]

"Do you view the Lord as a gracious God who desires your companionship?"

Time Set Apart

A friend and I were spending the day together. We ran errands and did some shopping. We also took time to stop, sit down, and just talk over tea. No matter what we did, we did it together. It is the same in our daily walk with the Lord. We can share with the Lord while cooking, driving, and working. To nurture a deeper intimacy, however, we need to spend focused, uninterrupted time with Him. I like Eugene Peterson's rendering of Jesus' words in Matthew 6:6: "Here's what I want you to do: Find a quiet, secluded place so you won't be tempted to role-play before God. Just be there as simply and honestly as you can manage. The focus will shift from you to God, and you will begin to sense his grace" (*The Message*).

We can't expect that we can receive all the teaching and refreshment we need on the run.

This "quiet" time with Him is a priority. It is essential to our journey because it nurtures our relationship with Him. We can't expect that we can receive all the teaching and refreshment we need on the run. Sitting at His feet provides the basis for communing with Him throughout the day. Reading His Word is part of listening to Him—in fact, it is a major dimension of prayer because if we are attentive, we will hear God speaking to us. This time with God doesn't require much of us—just quieting ourselves before Him, conversing with Him about what is on our hearts, and being simple and honest. It doesn't have to be a long session—but for whatever period of time we do have, it needs to be unhurried. David Brainerd described the richness of time set apart for the Lord:

> Enjoyed, I trust, the presence of God this morning in secret. O, how divinely sweet is it to come into the secret of his presence, and abide in his pavilion! . . . Time appeared but an inch long, and eternity at hand; and I thought I could with patience and cheerfulness bear any thing for the cause of God.[5]

So Brainerd was prepared for the day, whatever it might bring, because he spent time in prayer and meditation. It was out of his abiding that God used him mightily to take the gospel to the Native American tribes in the northeast United States. His real work lay in his times of secret pleading for the souls of the Native Americans. Out of his abiding came spiritual strength and guidance for how and where to serve.

Your fellowship with God does not necessarily guarantee a good day; it guarantees that you can get through the day to the glory of God.

Abiding does not negate service; it prepares you to be the woman God wants you to be, that He might use you for His purposes. Your fellowship with God does not necessarily guarantee a good day; it guarantees that you can get through the day to the glory of God.

"When do you set apart time for fellowship with your Guide?"

The Service of Adoration

Most of us think of serving as doing. Did Mary of Bethany serve Jesus in sitting quietly before Him? Absolutely! It was out of her communion with Him that she asked, "How can I show Jesus how much I love Him?" This is true service—showing Jesus how much we love Him.

I think that because Mary listened to Jesus, she was one of the few who really understood that He was about to die, and so she performed the act of devotion described in Mark's Gospel—lavishing expensive ointment on the Lord in a public display.

> *Most of us think of serving as doing. Did Mary of Bethany serve Jesus in sitting quietly before Him? Absolutely!*

Perhaps these were her thoughts: *Oh, Lord, You are the most precious One on earth to me. How can I communicate my devotion for You? How can I bless You? I know! I have an alabaster jar of lovely perfume. The least I can do is to anoint Your body for burial. And You will know how much I love You.*

Her service of adoration offended the disciples: "How can she do this? This is embarrassing and expensive. This perfume could be sold and the money given to the poor. Honestly, doesn't she know that this is not appropriate? Woman, leave us alone—you shouldn't even be here in the first place!"

But Jesus said,

Let her alone. Why are you giving her a hard time? She has just done something wonderfully significant for me. You will have the poor with you every day for the rest of your lives. Whenever you feel like it, you can do something for them. Not so with me. She did what she could when she could—she pre-anointed my body for burial. And you can be sure that wherever in the whole world the Message is preached, what she just did is going to be talked about admiringly. (Mark 14:6–9 *The Message*)

Oswald Chambers reflected on this adoration:

Have I ever been carried away to do something for God not because it was my duty, nor because it was useful, nor because there was anything in it at all beyond the fact that I love Him? . . . Not Divine, colossal things which could be recorded as marvelous, but ordinary, simple human things which will give evidence to God that I am abandoned to Him? Have I ever produced in the heart of the Lord Jesus what Mary of Bethany produced?[6]

I call that profound service. Mary's serving was an overflow, a natural product of her abiding. This is Jesus' teaching in John 15:5: "Yes, I am the vine; you are the branches. Those who remain in me, and I in them, will produce much fruit. For apart from me you can do nothing" (NLT).

Focused on One Thing

The young man was forced to go on a journey he did not want to take. He was in exile in a foreign country. He was thrust into a pagan culture and asked to conform to its practices. How was he to walk with and honor his God? How could he maintain his integrity in the midst of ungodliness? How could he fellowship with the Lord when a decree had been signed forbidding everyone from praying? The penalty for praying was death in a lions' den. Should he risk sacrificing his life to spend time with God? After all, the decree was only for a month. Surely, he could forgo a month—his very life was at stake.

What did he do? "When Daniel learned that the law had been signed, he went home and knelt down as usual in his upstairs room, with its windows open toward Jerusalem. He prayed three times a day, just as he had always done, giving thanks to his God" (Dan. 6:10 NLT).

Like Mary, Daniel believed that there is really only one thing worth being concerned about. Time with God and our communion with Him are *the* priorities. Ken Gire voices it well:

> I don't want to live in the kitchen of religious activity, distracted with all my preparations. I don't want to live slumped over some steamed-up stove, worried and upset about so many things. I want to live at the Savior's feet, gazing into His eyes, listening to His words.[7]

How remarkable to have a personal Guide on your journey—One who cares for your every need and who desires your companionship. He is patient and kind. He will protect you from everything on the path that will hinder you from reaching your destination. He knows exactly where you need to go, and He will lead you only to the places that are best for you. He is a perfect Guide. He longs to bring you closer to His heart.

> *I've found a Friend, O such a Friend!*
> *So kind, and true, and tender,*
> *So wise a Counselor and Guide,*
> *So mighty a Defender!*
> *From Him who loves me now so well,*
> *What power my soul can sever?*
> *Shall life or death, shall earth or hell?*
> *No! I am His forever.*[8]

SEVEN

The Guidebook

Until you can read the story of Adam and Eve, of Abraham and Sarah, of David and Bathsheba, as your own story . . . you have not really understood it. The Bible . . . is a book finally about ourselves, our own apostasies, our own battles and blessings.

Frederick Buechner[1]

When I travel to unfamiliar places, I buy a book or a pamphlet that tells me about my destination. I also find out the history of the city or country, the best way to travel, where to stay, what to eat, and what to see. These books are most helpful and informative. I find a travel guide to be indispensable.

For our journey, God has graciously provided His Word as our guidebook. The Bible is not a book that specifically tells us what to see each day or where to visit, but it gives us principles by which to travel, and stories of others who have made this pilgrimage. Since it is not tied to any single location, it transcends time and place. The Bible teaches us how to relate to others on the journey and how to stay on the path. But above all else, it tells us of our Father's heart. It is essentially the story of His love, provision, and sacrifice for His children. If we want to know our Father, we must know His Book. Its richest blessings are bestowed as we listen closely to the voice of our Guide speaking personally and lovingly through His Word.

Strength for the Journey

"I can't believe that all we get to eat is this *manna*—the same thing every day! And each morning we have to gather it all over again. Why can't we just collect a few days' worth, a couple of times a week? The other day I got a little more than I needed, and boy, did it ever spoil. My stomach still turns at the thought of how those worms looked. Okay, sure, it's nourishing, and although it's nothing to write home about, I'll admit it's satisfying. But morning after morning after morning we're up doing the same thing. I guess we have to if we want to stay alive and have strength to travel."

It is necessary to eat every day to maintain strength and energy. When we don't, our bodies weaken. The same is true with our spirits. To maintain spiritual strength, we must feed our spirits every day with the Word of God, our spiritual food. I think that God required the Israelites to gather manna every morning so that they would learn to come to Him daily.

I once heard someone observe that spiritual eating operates in the opposite way from physical eating. If we don't eat physically, we grow hungry. Once we consume food, the hunger subsides, and we feel satisfied. If we don't eat spiritually, we can lose our spiritual appetite. The less we eat spiritually, the less hungry we become. But the more we are nourished by the Word of God, the hungrier we become for spiritual food.

In another sense, however, the two forms of intake are alike. If you stop eating physically, you can count on family, friends, and medical professionals to urge or even coerce you into getting some food into you before you grow dangerously weak. They will know that the weaker you get, the less you may feel the desire to eat. I think this is true in the spiritual realm also. When you don't *feel* like reading the Scriptures (you're not getting anything out of it; you don't have the time; you're just not up for it), that is the very time you need to be sure to stay strong spiritually. Jesus' rebuke of Satan, while He was physically weak from fasting, illustrates this very point. Tempted to turn rocks into bread, the Lord responded by quoting the Scriptures, which gave Him spiritual strength to resist the devil's attack:

No! The Scriptures say,
"People need more than bread for their life;
they must feed on every word of God." (Matt. 4:4 NLT)

"How would you describe your appetite for God's Word?"

The Bible is *the* guidebook to the heart of God. It tells us everything we need to know about how to make this journey. It gives direction; it teaches; it corrects; it trains. It is God's Holy Spirit–breathed book for us to read, study, and meditate on. Through consistent intake of this, we will grow strong. Here we will find the revelation of our heavenly Father's character. Here we will discover His love for His people.

Every parent has heard the familiar excuse, "Oh, Mom, I didn't know you wanted me to do that!" We can never say to God, "I didn't know! If only You had told me!" All of His instructions are there in His Word, carefully preserved for our encouragement and use. It is really the only book we need on the trip. We can benefit, however, from the wisdom of other travelers regarding how best to mine its riches. I would like to share with you some insights that others have taught me, and that I have discovered firsthand to be very fruitful, about how to use the Bible to guide us in our journey to the heart of the Father.

A Reader's Delight

To spend time daily in the Scriptures, I have always used a yearly Bible reading plan. (Some people find it helpful to use a one-year Bible.) I need a schedule that tells me what to read on a specific day—and besides, if I didn't have a plan, I would never be likely to read Leviticus! I have found it important to be flexible. If I miss a day or two, I don't try to catch up; I go ahead and read the current day's selection. I may not read everything in a one-year plan, but I know that over a year's time, my reading will be much more consistent as a result.

If we don't eat spiritually, we can lose our spiritual appetite.

There is a place for studying the Bible, but I especially love just *reading* it. I'm not analyzing specific words, cross-referencing texts, or studying theology; I'm just reading. It's the Bible, me, and the Holy Spirit. I smiled when I heard someone comment, "The Bible is the only book in the world that when you read it, the Author shows up!" Jesus declared that the Spirit would be our Guide to the Guidebook: "But when the Father sends the Counselor as my representative—and by the Counselor I mean the Holy Spirit—he will teach you everything and will remind you of everything I myself have told you" (John 14:26 NLT).

John reinforced that declaration with the following assurance:

> You have received the Holy Spirit, and he lives within you, so you don't need anyone to teach you what is true. For the Spirit teaches you all things, and what he teaches is true—it is not a lie. So continue in what he has taught you, and continue to live in Christ. (1 John 2:27 NLT)

Does this mean I understand everything I read? Absolutely not. Having a study Bible or a commentary can be very helpful in explaining difficult passages. But when I read, I essentially open my Bible and pray very simply, "Open my eyes to see the wonderful truths in your law" (Ps. 119:18 NLT). I keep a journal in which I write down what I think God is saying to me in the Scriptures. I always try to learn something from what I read—an instruction I need to apply in my life, a comment concerning God's character and ways, or perhaps an example of how someone responded to Him.

For instance, each time I read the account of God's visit to Abraham and Sarah to tell them that the coming year would bring them a son, I usually write down how thankful I am that I cannot manipulate or fool

God. Sarah overheard the Lord telling Abraham the news, and she reacted with utter disbelief. The king and queen of senior citizens were going to have a baby? How impossible! She laughed to herself, and God called her on it:

> Then the LORD said to Abraham, "Why did Sarah laugh? Why did she say, 'Can an old woman like me have a baby?' Is anything too hard for the LORD?" . . . Sarah was afraid, so she denied that she had laughed. But [God] said, "That is not true. You did laugh." (Gen. 18:13–15 NLT)

God knew Sarah through and through, and He knows me. I am stripped of denial and deceit before Him. This story reaffirms for me that God always responds to His children in righteousness and truth. It reminds me of the power of His Word to place me before Him in total honesty: "For the word of God is full of living

The Bible is the guidebook to the heart of God.

power. It is sharper than the sharpest knife, cutting deep into our innermost thoughts and desires. It exposes us for what we really are" (Heb. 4:12 NLT).

"What can you do to increase your enjoyment of reading God's Word?"

The Bible's "living power" guarantees that it will always have fresh truth for my life. Someone has said, "The Word of God will stand a thousand readings, and he who has gone over it most frequently is the surest of finding new wonders there." Years ago I was reading Ruth, which at the time had already become one of my favorite books. As I read Ruth 3:11, I was struck by Boaz's declaration to her: "All my people in the city know that you are a woman of excellence" (NASB). I remember putting my Bible down and saying, "Lord, when did You put that verse in there? I never saw it before!"

A Treasure Trove for Study

Although reading the Bible is a source of great delight, I have found that studying it yields insights I would not discover by any other means. Paul exhorts us, "Do your utmost to let God see that you at least are a sound workman, with no need to be ashamed of the way you handle the word of the Truth" (2 Tim. 2:15 MOFFATT).

I remember putting my Bible down and saying, "Lord, when did You put that verse in there? I never saw it before!"

A "sound workman" who accurately handles the "word of the Truth" is a student of the Scriptures. The more we read the Word, the greater our hunger for deeper understanding of the riches it offers. I love the description of the Israelite priest: "The gracious hand of his God was on him. This was because Ezra had determined to study and obey the law of the LORD" (Ezra 7:9–10 NLT). Becoming a student of the Scriptures requires a determined desire to know and apply them.

A Scottish seminary professor was on holiday visiting an isolated village. As he took a stroll on a Sunday evening, he heard hymns being sung in a nearby church. He slipped inside the small building and took a seat in the back pew. When the singing stopped, an elderly weather-beaten farmer rose to speak. He opened his Bible and began to share from the Scriptures with humility, love, wisdom, and clarity. The professor was astounded at the man's comprehension of the Word. He was anxious to meet him and find out which seminary the man had attended.

After the service, the professor introduced himself and was invited to the farmer's home for tea. After some conversation, he asked the older gentleman where he had been taught to cultivate such discernment of the things of God. The older man went into his bedroom, knelt down at the foot of his bed, opened his Bible, and said, "This is where I study."

Whether you study the Scriptures alone or in a group, with a structured program or without, don't miss the riches that await you when you mine the depths of His Word, for they will lead straight to His heart.

Let the Word Dwell in Your Heart

Every morning before I get out of bed, I enjoy praying this Scripture to the Lord:

> My heart is steadfast, O God, my heart is steadfast;
> I will sing, yes, I will sing praises!
> Awake, my glory;
> Awake, harp and lyre,
> I will awaken the dawn!
> I will give thanks to Thee, O Lord, among the peoples;
> I will sing praises to Thee among the nations.
> For Thy lovingkindness is great to the heavens,
> And Thy truth to the clouds.
> Be exalted above the heavens, O God;
> Let Thy glory be above all the earth. (Ps. 57:7–11 NASB)

If I didn't have these verses committed to memory, I'd have to get myself up out of bed, fumble around to find my glasses, then get my Bible and turn to this passage, and read these wonderful verses to the Lord. But because I know them by heart, I can stay in bed a little longer!

I love Paul's instruction in Colossians 3:16: "Let the words of Christ, in all their richness, live in your hearts and make you wise" (NLT). Having the living Word in my heart is an essential part of my journey. I have found two primary motivators for "hiding" the Word in my heart.

First, *I memorize verses that I love.* Since the passage in Psalm 57 had always deeply moved me, one day I said, "Lord, I want to pray these verses to You each morning." So I began memorizing this passage until I could pray these precious words to the Lord first thing in the morning, straight from my heart to His.

Another passage that is special in my life is from Psalm 18. These verses are relevant for any and all situations; I could not travel anywhere without them:

> "I love Thee, O LORD, my strength."
> The LORD is my rock and my fortress and my deliverer,

My God, my rock, in whom I take refuge;
My shield and the horn of my salvation, my stronghold.
I call upon the LORD, who is worthy to be praised,
And I am saved from my enemies. (Ps. 18:1–3 NASB)

This passage takes my gaze off my circumstances and focuses it on God—the Lord is *my* rock, *my* fortress, *my* deliverer. These verses give me the strength and perspective I need to keep going. (How can anyone drive the freeways without these verses?!)

Second, *I memorize verses that I need*. For example, Paul's teaching in Ephesians 4:29 is an essential corrective for my speech: "Let no unwholesome word proceed from your mouth, but only such a word as is good for edification according to the need of the moment, that it may give grace to those who hear" (NASB).

Since I often speak before I think, I have memorized several verses concerning the tongue. For example, "I have hidden your word in my heart, that I might not sin against you" (Ps. 119:11 NLT). "When we have the Word in our hearts," it has been said, "the Holy Spirit has His own language with which to speak to us." So often after I have spoken an unwholesome word, the Holy Spirit reminds me of this verse. This prompting is 2 Timothy 3:16 in action: "All Scripture is inspired by God and is useful to teach us what is true and to make us realize what is wrong in our lives. It straightens us out and teaches us to do what is right" (NLT).

I find that I am more highly motivated to memorize verses that I love or need. I retain them more easily. I say them over and over with the desire to make them part of life. When I choose a verse to memorize, I write it on a 3" x 5" card. Then while I brush my teeth, dry my hair, cook, walk, wait at red lights, I commit the verse to memory. I carry these cards with me; I put them on the mirror; I place them on my desk. I keep them before me until they settle into my memory and dwell within my heart.

―――

"Are there any passages of Scripture you want to dwell within your heart while you are reading this book?"

―――

A Word for My Life

Every January, I ask the Lord what He wants to do in my life in the new year. What does He want to teach me? What needs to be changed? As I pray, either a need becomes very obvious or a verse is brought to my attention. When I realize my need—for example, my prayer life or my speech—I find an appropriate verse. I write the verse on a piece of paper the size of a bookmark, which I place in my Bible. I memorize the verse, and every day for a year I use the bookmark to prompt me to pray for that verse to become part of my life for the rest of my journey.

Don't miss the riches that await you when you mine the depths of His Word, for they will lead straight to His heart.

This practice has had an incredible impact on my life. God's Word is alive and active, and it penetrates and discloses my thoughts and motives. This year I am praying Proverbs 31:26 in *The Message* rendition: "When she speaks she has something worthwhile to say, and she always says it kindly." Certainly, this is a lifelong project, but my hope is that during this twelve-month period my speech might become a little more considerate, discreet, and discerning.

Dietrich Bonhoeffer, the twentieth-century Christian martyr who was executed for his resistance to the Nazi regime during World War II, called us to base our lives unswervingly on the Word of God:

> To deviate from the truth for the sake of some prospect of hope of our own can never be wise, however slight that deviation may be. It is not our judgement of the situation which can show us what is wise, but only the truth of the Word of God. Here alone lies the promise of God's faithfulness and help. It will always be true that the wisest course for the disciple is always to abide solely by the Word of God in all simplicity.[2]

I am convinced that the more time we spend in God's Word, the more we will understand Job's fervent declaration, "I have treasured the words of His mouth more than my necessary food" (Job 23:12 NASB). I read the Word of God, I study it, I memorize it, and I meditate on it because I love it, and because I want to grow and learn and be changed into His image. I do not consider this a spiritual discipline in the sense that it is something that *should* and *ought to* be done. I spend time with the Lord and His Word because doing so is the joy and delight of my heart. His Word is ever new, and His Spirit continually teaches and transforms me. Why would anything this world offers or demands keep me from the eternal richness and blessing of being with, and listening to, my Lord? This Guidebook is the ultimate guidebook, and it leads me straight to the heart of God.

> *Thou art the bread of life, O Lord, to me;*
> *Thy holy Word the truth that saveth me;*
> *Give me to eat and live*
> *With Thee above;*
> *Teach me to love Thy truth,*
> *For Thou art love.*[3]

EIGHT

A
Passionate
Reverence

In knots, to be loosed never
Knit my heart to thee for ever.
That I to thy name may bear
Fearful love and loving fear.

Francis Davison[1]

S ome of us are passionate about certain locations, and we travel to them as often as we can. The ocean fascinates me; I can sit for hours on a rock and contemplate the vastness and mystery of this hidden world. When I am home in Tucson, I am again in a place that surrounds me with the uniqueness of God's creation.

Extraordinary places beckon us to stand literally in awe as we contemplate their unique beauty. They call to us like no other destination, evoking powerful longings.

The more we draw near to the heart of God, the more we discover how powerfully we long for the eternal—for it is there that we see perfect beauty and holiness. Just as we return repeatedly to a place we love, so we will return continually to stand in awe of Him. This is passionate reverence for God.

To Fear Him Above All

What was he to do? This time it was different; he was all alone in the house with her. And she was after him again—pressuring him to sleep with her. His master's wife! He had refused her so many times. "How could I ever do such a wicked thing?" he had exclaimed to her. "I would be committing a great sin against God." He tried never to be where she was, but now he was trapped.

> *If we don't fear God, our lives will lead us toward compromise, emptiness, and presumption.*

Would it really matter if he stayed with her? Would anyone ever know? She grabbed his shirt. And Joseph tore himself away and ran. (See Gen. 39.)

Why did Joseph run? Because he feared God. The writer of Proverbs tells us that "The fear of the LORD is the beginning of knowledge" (Prov. 1:7 NASB). Joseph's knowledge of right and wrong was rooted in God's commands. His decision to act on that knowledge was rooted in his reverence for the Lord.

If we don't fear God, our lives will lead us toward compromise, emptiness, and presumption. We will journey here without the knowledge of God we so urgently need in order to live as He created us and desires us to live. He has given us our very existence. We are His idea, His chosen, His children. To reverence and to honor Him above all place us in a position to receive His wisdom, enabling us to experience His purpose and fulfillment.

After his great declaration regarding the fear of the Lord in the first part of 1:7, the writer of Proverbs reinforced it by adding, "Fools despise wisdom and instruction." Indeed, it is foolish to think that I have all wisdom and I don't need to be taught. Jesus taught, "God blesses those who realize their need for him, for the Kingdom of Heaven is given to them" (Matt. 5:3 NLT).

Oswald Chambers asserted, "When you fear God you fear nothing else."[2] It is incredibly freeing to understand that the only fear we should have is for our God. Jesus spoke very clearly on this point: "Don't be afraid of those who want to kill you. They can only kill your body; they cannot touch your soul. Fear only God, who can destroy both soul and body in hell" (Matt. 10:28 NLT). Eugene Peterson renders this verse in *The Message*, "Don't be bluffed into silence by the threats of bullies. There's nothing they can do to your soul, your core being. Save your fear for God, who holds your entire life—body and soul—in his hands."

We fear a God who loves and redeems, but who also judges and is sovereign. He, and He alone, wields power for eternity:

> I, even I, am the LORD;
> And there is no savior besides Me. . . .
> Even from eternity I am He;
> And there is none who can deliver out of My hand;
> I act and who can reverse it? (Isa. 43:11, 13 NASB)

God is the One with authority. He is the only authority to whom we will answer for the way we have lived. If we fear God, then we are free from other fears. King David sang joyfully in this truth:

> In God, whose word I praise,
> In God I have put my trust;
> I shall not be afraid.
> What can mere man do to me? (Ps. 56:4 NASB)

Think of the Israelites spending their lives wandering in the wilderness, fearing man instead of God. Joseph's reverence was reserved for God—not for Potiphar, Potiphar's wife, or the consequences that might result from his rejection of her.

―――

"What do you think is the difference between fearing God and being afraid of God?"

―――

When you fear God, you will be freed to listen to His "fear nots." Prayerfully read each of these assurances, asking God to enable you by His Spirit to receive the comfort He offers in them (emphasis added):

Do not fear, for I am with you. (Isa. 41:10 NASB)

For I am the LORD your God, who upholds your right hand,
Who says to you, *"Do not fear,* I will help you." (Isa. 41:13
   NASB)

Do not fear, for I have redeemed you;
I have called you by name; you are Mine! (Isa. 43:1 NASB)

Listen to Me, you who know righteousness,
A people in whose heart is My law;
Do not fear the reproach of man,
Neither be dismayed at their revilings. (Isa. 51:7 NASB)

Indeed, the very hairs of your head are all numbered. *Do not fear;*
you are of more value than many sparrows. (Luke 12:7 NASB)

Fearing God means living purely and obediently. Fearing God is understanding that God is the only One worthy of reverence and awe. Fearing God means we may be set free from all other fears.

Portrait of a Woman Who Fears God

The example of the godly woman in Proverbs 31 continues to have a profound influence in my life. She is always available as an excellent role model. It is easy to view her as extremely talented, very busy—and perfect! Not so: we know she was an imperfect human being, and it's unlikely that she could have been any busier than we are today. Her life is summed up in verse 30: "Charm is deceptive, and beauty does not last; but a woman who fears the LORD will be greatly praised" (NLT).

What did she do that was so outstanding? Let's take a look. We can see that she took care of her family, her home, herself. She had maidens to help her, but so do we—dishwashers, washing machines, dryers, microwaves, and so forth, but without any emotional problems! She was organized and used her talent to help out financially. She was concerned about others in need—physically as well as spiritually. She liked to look nice. Sounds like a nineties' woman to me!

So what else did she do that earned her star billing from the Proverbs writer? What made her so special that her worth was "far above rubies" (v. 10 AMPLIFIED)?

A closer look reveals what made her virtuous and excellent. The bottom line of her life was that she feared God. Because she feared God, she ministered well to her family. The family can include parents, husband, children, siblings, loved ones—anyone we are very close to, who trusts in us for care. She did her best to encourage the people she was intimate with and responsible for, and to serve them for their good. Certainly, she knew that one day she would give account of how she related to those whom God had entrusted to her.

> *If we fear God, then we are free from other fears.*

Because she feared God, she was organized. The fact that her lamp was always burning meant that she had enough oil to keep it lit through the night. Some write that this was a sign of hospitality to strangers— and therefore it is not a commendation that she stayed up late, but that she was prepared to extend herself to others. I've thought that in my case, this would mean that I always had milk for breakfast!

She was disciplined, which means that she didn't slack off by eating "the bread of idleness" (v. 27 NASB). Instead of viewing her as a perfectionist who never stopped, I think that because of her desire to honor God, she never allowed anything to come into her life that would compromise her walk with the Lord.

Because she feared God, she took care of herself: "She girds herself with strength, / And makes her arms strong" (v. 17 NASB). She knew the importance of keeping herself strong physically as well as spiritually in order to carry out God's purposes.

Because this woman feared God, she was sensitive to those in need. I like the placement of this verse (v. 20) because she had already taken care of her family, home, and herself—then she reached out compassionately to serve others beyond her immediate family.

Because she feared God, she dressed appropriately and tastefully. One translation says that she wore "fine linen and purple" (v. 22 NASB). (Since the fine linen was white and she dressed in purple, I've decided that her color season was winter!) Again, her desire to please God motivated everything she did, even in the kind of clothing she chose to wear.

> *I fear Him by continually standing in awe of His holy and just character.*

But it was not just her outward appearance that she clothed. She had to have had a strong walk with God because her inward adornment was strength, courage, and perseverance. She was gracious and honorable. Other evidence of her fear of the Lord was her speech: it was wise and kind. Out of the abundance of the heart the mouth speaks, and so her heart must have been filled with God's wisdom for her speech to have been characterized by discernment and consideration. Because she feared God, she did not fear anything else, not even the future.

*"What gives you strength spiritually and physically?
Do you pursue it out of fear and reverence for the Lord?"*

Standing in Awe of God

Robert Nisbet depicts the fear of God in the posture of a rebel readmitted to the throne room of a benevolent ruler:

> It is the fear which a child feels toward an honored parent—a fear to offend; it is that which they who have been rescued from destruction feel to the benefactor who nobly and at sacrifice interposed for their safety—a fear to act unworthily of his kindness: it is that which fills the breast of a pardoned and grateful rebel in the presence of a venerated sovereign at whose throne he is permitted

to stand in honor—a fear lest he should ever forget his goodness and give him cause to regret it. Such is the fear of the Christian now: a fear which reverence for majesty, gratitude for mercies, dread of displeasure, desire of approval, and longing for the fellowship of heaven, inspire.[3]

At times, fearing God seems to be a weighty responsibility. But Scripture has much to say regarding its benefits and delights:

When we fear God, He grants us a special intimacy with Him:

Friendship with the LORD is reserved for those who fear him.
    With them he shares the secrets of his covenant. (Ps. 25:14 NLT)

"Why do you think the psalmist connects fear of God and friendship with God?"

Fearing God opens us to experience His fatherly love:

The LORD is like a father to his children,
    tender and compassionate to those who fear him. (Ps. 103:13 NLT)

Fear of God is the foundation for a satisfying life:

Charm is deceptive, and beauty does not last; but a woman who fears the LORD will be greatly praised. (Prov. 31:30 NLT)

My fear of God is rooted in love and reverential respect for Him. I do not fear God out of dread or apprehension of His judgment or apparent sternness. I fear Him by continually standing in awe of His holy and just character. This motivates me to live in a manner that brings Him honor and pleasure, for I must give an account of my life to Him. Knowing that one day I will stand before my Father, who sent His Son to die for me, who lavishes His grace and Holy Spirit upon me, who is always *for* me, who works within me to accomplish His purposes, who loves me unconditionally, who considers me worthy to be called His child—knowing that intensifies my longing to please Him, revere His name, and bring Him glory.

How can I stand before the living God and be ashamed of not loving, obeying, and trusting Him enough? I don't want to offend God; I don't want to act unworthily of His name; I don't ever want to forget His goodness to me. So my fear, my passionate reverence, of Him impels me to this destination that draws me like no other.

My fear, my passionate reverence, of Him impels me to this destination that draws me like no other.

May your reverence of God draw you ever closer to His heart, to stand in awe of His majesty, beauty, and peace.

> *For Thyself, best gift divine,*
> *To our race so freely given;*
> *For that great, great love of Thine,*
> *Peace on earth and joy in heaven;*
> *Lord of all, to Thee we raise*
> *This our hymn of grateful praise.*[4]

NINE

Stay on the Path

The essential thing "in heaven and earth" is . . .
that there should be a long obedience in the same
direction; there thereby results, and has always
resulted in the long run, something which has
made life worth living.

Friedrich Nietzsche[1]

After my mom decided that having me along as a tour companion was sufficiently successful to repeat the experience, she asked me to accompany her to Spain. While we were on a special tour and visiting a museum, a couple in our group decided to leave and find a coffee shop—without telling our tour guide. When it was time for us to depart to another city, the two could not be found. We waited as long as possible, but since we were on a schedule, we eventually had to leave without them. It took two days for the couple to rejoin us. They did not speak Spanish, and they encountered numerous difficulties when arranging transportation and lodging on their own. After much frustration and considerable expenditure, they caught up with us. After that, they were very obedient and punctual members of our tour!

Scripture is straightforward about our need to "stay on the path" in our journey with the Lord:

> Happy are those who obey his decrees
> and search for him with all their hearts.
> They do not compromise with evil,
> and they walk only in his paths. (Ps. 119:2–3 NLT)

Sometimes, however, the rewards of staying the course seem few and far between. Joseph refused to violate God's commands and yield to the attempts of Potiphar's wife to seduce him. What happened next? She falsely accused him of attacking her, and he was promptly thrown into a dungeon for several years. He had not compromised with evil, but look where it got him! He lost his job, and he was stuck in a prison. Was he happy— or blessed, as other translations render Psalm 119:2—for obeying God and for walking only in His paths?

> *Joseph trusted God, even when it looked as if he would spend the rest of his life in prison.*

Here I think of Psalm 37:16: "It is better to be godly and have little than to be evil and possess much" (NLT). Yes, I think Joseph was "happy" that he obeyed. I don't think he was terribly pleased with his circumstances, but better to have a clear conscience before God in prison than to live in unrighteousness in Potiphar's house. Does obedience bring blessing? Let's see. . . .

When the Blessing Is a Long Time in Coming

It is just another day in a long line of days in prison. He gets up off the floor in the same dungeon . . . the same clothes . . . to the same food . . . and the same routine . . . and always the same darkness.

Then the silence is broken by the sounds of men scurrying about, talking loudly—to him. "Hurry, hurry, Joseph! You must shave. You must change your clothes. You must appear before Pharaoh!"

Suddenly, Joseph is thrust into Pharaoh's presence. Pharaoh tells Joseph of a vivid dream he had the night before, and Joseph interprets it.

In a whirl of activity, Joseph looks down at his hand and notices Pharaoh's signet ring on his finger. He feels a gold chain being placed around his neck. Fine linen clothes adorn his body. He rides in a chariot behind Pharaoh, and everyone bows to him. In a few hours, he has gone from prison to prime minister. Does God bless obedience in the midst of a harsh and unforgiving world? Talk to Joseph.

But Joseph's journey to a gold necklace took about thirteen years—thirteen *hard* years. Why did God delay the blessing? The psalmist provides a clue:

> He called for a famine on the land of Canaan,
>   cutting off its food supply.
> Then he sent someone to Egypt ahead of them—
>   Joseph, who was sold as a slave.
> There in prison, they bruised his feet with fetters
>   and placed his neck in an iron collar.
> Until the time came to fulfill his word,
>   the LORD tested Joseph's character. (Ps. 105:16–19 NLT)

I can't help thinking, *Lord, Joseph had quite a test! Was it really necessary?* But God had chosen him for an assignment that would require incredible wisdom and discernment in living in a corrupt society. Joseph needed to attend a "school" that would train him in administration, servanthood, holiness, and dependency upon his God. And Joseph trusted God, even when it looked as if he would spend the rest of his life in prison. As his trust was tried, his character was molded. He graduated from this school ready for the purpose and plan God had for him and his people. God meant all of it for *good*. Those thirteen long years, God knew the blessing and honor that Joseph would receive. He just needed to be sure Joseph was prepared.

"When has God tested your obedience,
and how has it strengthened you?"

"A delayed blessing tests men," Charles Spurgeon commented, "and proves their mettle, whether their faith is of that precious kind which can endure the fire."[2]

Peter explains God's purposes in allowing us to go through extended times of difficulty:

> These trials are only to test your faith, to show that it is strong and pure. It is being tested as fire tests and purifies gold—and your faith is far more precious to God than mere gold. So if your faith remains strong after being tried by fiery trials, it will bring you much praise and glory and honor on the day when Jesus Christ is revealed to the whole world. (1 Peter 1:7 NLT)

This is how I felt during our days in Temple, Texas: "Lord, what is happening to me? Three children in three years. You know that I'm not a baby-person. I'm essentially an only child. My brother is six and a half years younger than I am. I'm not used to constant chaos! Two in diapers plus a toddler—it takes me half a day just to grocery shop! I don't like trying to remember whose turn it is to have the blue bowl. And I can't cool three bowls of Cream of Wheat at the same time. Going somewhere is a major event. I need an oversized suitcase to pack everything necessary for three small children. There's no time to do anything I want to do . . . like sleep, and maybe even finish a complete sentence. In my most tired moments I feel a kindred spirit with Joseph, who was a slave and in prison."

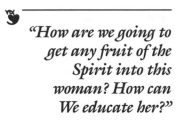

"How are we going to get any fruit of the Spirit into this woman? How can We educate her?"

As I look back over my life, a major testing of my faith came with our three children, and a few years later, a fourth. (Then there was the period later on when we had four teenagers all at once.) I think God had looked down at me and said, "How are We going to get any fruit of the Spirit into this woman? How can We educate her? I know. We'll send her to the School of Instant and Constant Motherhood. This is a good curriculum for teaching total dependence, patience, kindness, self-control, love—all the fruit of My Spirit. She doesn't know it, but I'm preparing her to be an older woman in My kingdom. Let's see if she passes the test."

❦

Obeying God's commands is always for our benefit. Moses told Israel that God wanted them to obey the Lord's commands for their own good (Deut. 10:13). We instruct small children not to touch a hot stove. We make it very clear that they may play in the yard, but never in the street. Why? For their health and safety. So it is with us. When God asks us to obey, it is for our good.

――――

"Where in your life is God asking you to obey?
Do you believe it is for your good?"

――――

Obey Now
or Pay Later

Simon Peter, Andrew, James, and John had fished all night and caught nothing. Simon, in particular, was greatly disheartened. He painstakingly washed the nets and was almost ready to go home and collapse in fatigue when Jesus showed up, with the multitudes following Him. The Rabbi climbed into Simon's boat and asked him to push away from the shore, so He could have just enough distance from the press of the crowd to teach. Simon must have thought, *Oh, no. I'm so tired, and now I'm in the boat with Jesus. I wonder how long He will teach?*

Obedience is believing that God knows what He is asking, that He gives strength to obey, and that it is always for our good.

When Jesus finished, He asked Simon to go out into the deep water and let down the nets for a catch. Here is my paraphrased version of Simon's response: "Lord, we have fished all night, and I want You to know that I can testify there are NO fish in this lake!" (Luke 5:5). (*The Message* renders it, "Master, we've been fishing hard all night and haven't caught even a minnow.")

I imagine that Simon went on to say, "In fact, Lord, this is not the time to fish. It's getting hot, and besides, I'm really tired. I know You know about carpentry, but I'm not sure You know much about fishing. But IF YOU INSIST, I'll let down the nets."

I love this Scripture because I identify with Simon. Often, I am tired and just glad to be home. Then out of the blue, here's Jesus with a request. Will you visit this person? Will you be hospitable to these people I'm sending your way? "But, Lord, I've been with people. I need some rest! Go out into the deep and let down my nets? Okay, if You really want me to." This is obedience. Obedience is simply saying, "Yes, I'll let down *my* nets and do Your bidding." Obedience is believing that God knows what He is asking, that He gives strength to obey, and that it is always for our good. (Be on the alert: obedience can also bring an abundance of fish where you thought the waters were empty!)

What I find interesting in all examples of disobedience in the Scriptures is, Guess who is always right? Guess who pays the price?

Just as there is blessing in obedience, so there are serious consequences in disobedience. The couple who strayed from our tour paid a high cost financially and emotionally. When we do not stay on the path, we, too, pay a price:

> "Run for your lives!" the angels warned. "Do not stop anywhere in the valley. *And don't look back!* Escape to the mountains, or you will die." . . . But Lot's wife looked back as she was following along behind him, and she became a pillar of salt. (Gen. 19:17, 26 NLT, italics added)

The command was clear. Her disobedience cost the woman her life.

God told Jonah, "Get up and go to the great city of Nineveh! Announce my judgment against it because I have seen how wicked its people are." Jonah listened to God's command, and then he "went in the opposite direction in order to get away from the LORD" (Jonah 1:2–3 NLT).

In consequence of Jonah's disobedience, "the LORD had arranged for a great fish to swallow Jonah. And Jonah was inside the fish for three days and three nights" (Jonah 1:17 NLT).

When we're feeling salty or we find ourselves in the belly of a whale, we probably need to take an obedience check. What I find interesting in these examples—and indeed, in all examples of disobedience in the Scriptures—is, Guess who is always right? Guess who pays the price? When God speaks, our refusal exacts a high cost and can easily lead to long-range consequences.

I am often prompted by the Holy Spirit to call someone, write a note of encouragement, or visit with a friend. The prompting is very distinct: a name is brought to my mind with the suggestion to move toward that person in some way. I usually respond by mentally agreeing with this prodding—but more often than not, I fail to follow through. Then a few days later, I'll hear that this person had been struggling. She needed prayer and a word of assurance. The price I pay is missing out on the blessing of ministering to a friend, of helping her bear her burden, of participating with the Lord in His work.

The Danger of a Heart Divided

"If you love Me, you will keep My commandments," Jesus said (John 14:15 NASB). The clarity and the simplicity of His teaching on obedience are very convicting. If we love others, we want to please them. If we love Jesus, we will please Him by obeying. What has He asked us to do? Love God with all of our hearts, souls, and minds, and love our neighbor as ourselves. It is an incredible commentary on our selfishness that we have to be commanded to love God, who is Love. But the way we know—and the way God knows—that we love Him is by our *wholehearted* obedience to Him.

King Saul is a prime example of how halfhearted obedience displeases God. Samuel conveyed a message to Saul direct from the Lord: "I have decided to settle accounts with the nation of Amalek for opposing Israel when they came from Egypt. Now go and completely destroy the entire

Amalekite nation—men, women, children, babies, cattle, sheep, camels, and donkeys" (1 Sam. 15:2–3 NLT).

Later on we learn of Saul's response: "Saul and his men spared Agag's [the king's] life and kept the best of the sheep and cattle, the fat calves and lambs—everything, in fact, that appealed to them. They destroyed only what was worthless or of poor quality" (1 Sam. 15:9 NLT). I want to ask Saul, "What is it about the words *completely destroy* that you don't understand?" Apparently, the Lord felt the same way.

Samuel rebuked Saul, "Why haven't you obeyed the LORD? Why did you rush for the plunder and do exactly what the LORD said not to do?"

Poor Saul replied, "But I did obey the LORD. . . . My troops brought in the best of the sheep and cattle and plunder to sacrifice to the LORD your God in Gilgal."

> *She certainly didn't know what lay ahead, but she did know that she trusted God.*

Then came Samuel's piercing reply: "What is more pleasing to the LORD: your burnt offerings and sacrifices or your obedience to his voice? Obedience is far better than sacrifice" (1 Sam. 15:19, 20–22 NLT).

Saul's ultimate reason for disobeying was that he was afraid of the people, and he did what *they* demanded. Another one who feared people instead of God. If we truly reverence God, we will not allow our obedience to Him to be sacrificed by a divided heart.

"Is your heart divided between pleasing God and pleasing people?"

I am still in the process of learning obedience instead of sacrifice. Often when I am asked to serve on a committee, teach a class, bake ten dozen cookies, or phone a list of people for a meeting, I automatically say yes. There is nothing wrong in doing any of these things if I do them in obedience to the Lord. I tend to presume that since this is a *good* thing, then it must mean that I should do it. Like Saul, I like to do what people ask. But when I say yes for the wrong reasons, it usually happens that I end up *sacrificing* my family, my time, and my patience to fulfill the obligation.

Instead of asking God for His will ahead of time, I find myself saying afterward, "But, Lord, this is for You. Aren't You pleased?" The Lord replies, *Obedience is far better than sacrifice.*

Mary, the mother of Jesus, gives us a picture of love and reverence of God. She spoke to Gabriel the most beautiful words expressing whole-hearted obedience: "I am the Lord's servant, and I am willing to accept whatever he wants. May everything you have said come true" (Luke 1:38 NLT). She didn't fully understand all the implications of her obedience, and she certainly didn't know what lay ahead, but she did know that she trusted God. She wanted to obey Him by walking in His chosen paths.

Staying on the path is essential for your journey. It is imperative to be continually alert to His commands and promptings, for straying from His path can have lasting, unpleasant consequences. Offering to God an obedient heart pleases Him and brings good into your life as you journey. Trusting Him to know what is best for you helps you to obey. When you reach your destination, you will not regret having stayed on the path. Obedience out of love for God brings great reward.

"Wait passionately for GOD, don't leave the path" (Ps. 37:34 *The Message*).

O Jesus, I have promised
To serve Thee to the end;
Be Thou forever near me,
My Master and my Friend;
I shall not fear the battle
If Thou art by my side,
Nor wander from the pathway
If Thou wilt be my Guide.[3]

TEN

Righteous Clothing

How little people know who think that holiness
is dull.

C. S. Lewis[1]

Having the proper clothing on a trip is very important. It is always hard
for me to pack because I live in a warm climate and I must often go
where it is much colder. Once I left Tucson in August to travel to New
Zealand, where it was winter. After the first few engagements, I began to
smile as I heard the same thing said of me each time I proceeded to a new
location. Whenever anyone had to meet me, he or she was told, "Look
for the woman with the long black wool coat, gloves, and pink muf-
fler." I was glad to have every piece of my winter clothing, for I surely
needed it. Wearing clothes that are appropriate for the climate and sur-
roundings makes the journey all the more enjoyable.

Does God
Ask Us to Do
the Impossible?

Peter describes the spiritual apparel necessary to journey to the heart of
God: "But now you must be holy in everything you do, just as God—who

chose you to be his children—is holy. For he himself has said, 'You must be holy because I am holy'" (1 Peter 1:15–16 NLT).

In ancient Greek culture there was a race in which the winner was not necessarily the one who reached the finish line first, but the one who crossed the finish line with his torch burning. This is a good illustration of living a holy life—arriving at our final destination with our torch burning. I want to meet the Lord with my life as unblemished as possible; I desire to be morally pure, blameless in my heart and life. The closer I travel toward His heart, the more I sense His holiness and His great longing for me to exemplify holiness as His child.

> *God does not ask us to be holy because He is a stern taskmaster. He asks us to be holy because He loves us.*

To be holy in *everything* I do is an incredibly high standard. It is a rather daunting, seemingly impossible, command to obey. Oswald Chambers's explanation is helpful here:

> It is quite true to say—"I cannot live a holy life," but you can decide to let Jesus Christ make you holy. . . . Redemption means that Jesus Christ can put into any man the hereditary disposition that was in Himself, and all the standards He gives are based on that disposition: *His teaching is for the life He puts in.* The moral transaction on my part is agreement with God's verdict on sin in the Cross of Jesus Christ.[2]

Because of Christ, I have been declared righteous before God: "He made Him who knew no sin to be sin on our behalf, that we might become the righteousness of God in Him" (2 Cor. 5:21 NASB). Because of the Holy Spirit in me, I can be Christlike.

Why does God command holiness, especially in a world that promotes everything but purity? It's not easy to be holy—and, we think, it's no fun! Unfortunately, there is pleasure in sin for a season. But it is only a season, and then we must live with the sometimes disabling ramifications of our indulgence. God does not want us to suffer the unnecessary consequences of sin. To those who have not pursued holiness in the past: be assured of 1 John 1:9—"But if we confess our sins to him, he is faithful and just to forgive us and to cleanse us from every wrong" (NLT).

Although we live in a world terribly distorted by sin, we are no longer slaves to sin, and we can yield ourselves to righteousness. Peter assured us, "His divine power gives us everything we need for living a godly life. . . . He has promised that you will escape the decadence all around you caused by evil desires and that you will share in his divine nature" (2 Peter 1:3–4 NLT). God has given us His example, His Spirit, and His Word. We cannot stand before Him and say, "Your command for me to be holy was totally unreasonable. After all, I was only human." God does not ask us to be holy because He is a stern taskmaster. He asks us to be holy because He loves us. He knows that sharing in His divine nature is supremely more fulfilling and satisfying than sharing in anything the world offers.

> *I will never be perfectly holy, but my part is to want to travel on the highway of holiness.*

"Can you affirm that the blessing of purity is far greater than the pleasures of the world?"

Choosing to Put on Righteous Clothing

Once I understand God's part in calling me to become holy, what is my part in pursuing holiness? How can I always be dressed suitably on my journey? How can I stay "stain-free"?

One of the primary tenets of successful dieting, especially when dining out, is to decide ahead of time what you will eat. The chances of maintaining your diet are a lot better if you mentally commit to staying on your regimen. If you wait to decide until you get to a restaurant and hear what others are ordering, you may yield to temptation and decide to postpone the diet until the next day!

The same principle is true spiritually. A commitment or decision made before the Lord will go a long way in helping us stay true to that promise when we are tempted. Chambers commented, "The battle is lost or won in the secret places of the will before God, never first in the external world. . . . Nothing has any power over the man who has fought out the battle before God and won there."[3]

"The essence of holiness," it has been said, "is not that we are perfect, but that we never stop pursuing it." I will never be perfectly holy, but my part is to *want* to travel on the highway of holiness. My part is to take responsibility for my decisions and actions. I yield to temptation because of my desire to do so. The power of sin is broken in my life, so the choice is mine: sin or righteousness?

Years ago I discovered the freedom and power of making *predecisions* in regard to holiness. These decisions have blessed me and helped me immensely in guarding my purity. As an older woman whom Scripture exhorts to teach purity to younger women, I share them with you. They are not legalisms, but guidelines I have adopted so that, I hope, I can keep my torch burning. They are born out of my weakness because I know my sinful heart too well.

Relating to Men

Predecision #1: I will guard against emotional adultery by taking every thought captive to the obedience of Christ. "We use our powerful God-tools for smashing warped philosophies, tearing down barriers erected against the truth of God, fitting every loose thought and emotion and impulse into the structure of life shaped by Christ" (2 Cor. 10:5 *The Message*).

When she yielded to temptation, Eve began by *seeing* that the tree was good; then she *desired* it. That was the beginning of her fall. If I am married, I cannot look at or desire other men. If I am single, I cannot desire a married man. Jesus taught, "Your *heart* can be corrupted by lust even quicker than your *body*. Those leering looks you think nobody notices—they also corrupt" (Matt. 5:28 *The Message*).

So every time I have an impure thought about another man, I have predetermined to take it captive. I put that thought in "prison" and then make my thoughts obedient to Christ. I do not entertain this "loose" thought; I disarm it. Deciding ahead of time to do this enables the Holy Spirit to prompt and strengthen me, making it easier for me to obey.

Predecision #2: As much as it depends on me, since I am married, I will never be alone with another man in a social situation. (If you are single, your decision would be never to be alone with a married man in a social situation.)

The idea behind this resolution is that if I'm not alone with another man, how can I ever commit adultery? Now, I'm aware of many exceptions. What if I'm working and have to have dinner with another man? What if I'm traveling and I have no choice? That's why the first part of the decision is "as much as it depends on me."

> *Peter warned of this danger, "Keep a cool head. Stay alert. The Devil is poised to pounce."*

Shortly after I made this decision (which I thought was a little presumptuous because other men never asked me to be alone with them!), a well-meaning pastor asked me if I would have lunch with him. He wanted to talk with me about women's ministry and ask me some questions about women's needs. Now I didn't say, "Well, that's nice of you to ask, but because I'm pursuing holiness, I cannot have lunch with you!" I replied, "Oh, I appreciate your invitation. Would you mind if I bring a friend who has good insights concerning women?" (I took Jack, my husband.)

On one occasion when I arrived to speak at a seminar, I was picked up by the husband of the woman organizing the event. His wife was teaching school. It was lunchtime, and we stopped to eat. I had no choice, and that's okay. But I was alert and very aware of wanting to be God's woman with pure thoughts and motives.

Several brokenhearted women have told me that their affairs always began very innocently, usually with lunch. No one starts out by saying, "Let's have lunch so we can sin and tear two families apart." Peter warns of this danger, "Keep a cool head. Stay alert. The Devil is poised to pounce, and would like nothing better than to catch you napping. Keep your guard up" (1 Peter 5:8 *The Message*). Making this predecision has been a major way of keeping my guard up.

Predecision #3: I will give only holy hugs and kisses to other men. Paul closed one of his letters by saying, "Greet one another with a holy kiss" (Rom. 16:16 NASB). As members of the body of Christ, we are brothers and sisters. It is good to greet one another. But the kiss and hug I give my brother are different from the kiss and hug I give my husband. I made this predecision because I have received some hugs that I sensed were not entirely holy. At different times, we are all needy and can be very vulnerable. Again, innocent hugs or kisses can lead to an occasion for the enemy to pounce. Determining to give holy hugs is another way of keeping up our guard. I've concluded that the best hug to give a brother in Christ is a *side* hug. When I see a full body hug approaching, I put my left hand on the man's right shoulder, my right hand pats his back, and we greet each other without our bodies touching.

"Are there any predecisions you need to make regarding your relationships with men?"

Activities

Predecision #4: I will try not to read, watch, or listen to anything that would grieve the Holy Spirit who lives within me. I once noticed a young person wearing a T-shirt that had emblazoned on it, "How much can I get away with and still get to heaven?" Unfortunately, that is an earnest question in today's world, even among some believers. With our culture becoming more blatantly sinful, it is easy to begin to subtly compromise our perception of what holiness really looks like. Jeremiah made this statement about the nation of Judah: "They did not know how to blush" (Jer. 8:12 NASB). The same could be said about us and our society.

> *We cannot expect to make steady progress on our spiritual journey if we insist on taking little side trips away from the highway of holiness.*

We are told in Hebrews 12:1 that as we run our race, we are to lay aside the "sin which so easily entangles us" (NASB). Sin is our competitor. It will look for ways to trip us up and take us out of the race. As I was praying and asking God to show me how I could keep from being entangled by sin, I found this verse:

> Don't let me lust for evil things;
> don't let me participate in acts of wickedness.

Don't let me share in the delicacies of those who do evil.
(Ps. 141:4 NLT)

I am not plagued with lust for evil things, nor do I desire to participate in deeds of wickedness, but this verse revealed to me how easily I share the *delicacies* of sin. Another translation says, "And do not let me eat of their delicacies" (NASB). Although I do not necessarily practice wickedness, I do take little nibbles around the delicacies of sin.

John Wesley's mother is said to have written to him when he was in college, "Would you judge of the lawfulness of a pleasure, take this rule: whatever weakens your reason, impairs the tenderness of your conscience, obscures your sense of God, or takes away the relish of spiritual things; whatever increases the authority of your body over your mind, that thing is sin."

I like these guidelines for choosing my activities. Predetermining that I will not partake of any form of entertainment that will obscure my sense of God is very freeing. I don't have to debate or struggle. Most of the time the choice is very clear.

C. S. Lewis observed that holiness is not dull. It's true. I enjoy the classics—literature, music, and movies. Some modern authors do not impair the tenderness of my conscience, and there are many Christian novels from which to choose. I do not have to eat the delicacies of sin to be entertained.

It is paramount that we guard our hearts with all diligence. To guard with all diligence means to maintain constant vigilance—continual watchfulness. We do not "deserve a break" from pursuing holiness. William Gurnall, a Puritan author, wrote, "This is your calling: to make the Christian faith your daily work, without any vacation from one end of the year to the other."[4] We cannot expect to make steady progress on our spiritual journey if we insist on taking little side trips away from the highway of holiness.

═══

"Are there any predecisions you need to make regarding your leisure activities?"

═══

A Growing
Sensitivity

A word to keep from being discouraged: the longer I am on this journey, the more I am beginning to understand Paul's statement that he was the chief of all sinners. Paul made the comment when he was near the end of his life—his journey was almost complete. I have come to realize that the more intimate I become with the Lord, the more sensitive I become to sin in my own life.

The first time I discovered Psalm 17:3, "I have purposed that my mouth will not transgress" (NASB), I prayed that this verse would come true in my life. But after that, my tongue went on a rampage—I was critical, irritable, and snippy. I ran back to the Lord and asked why was it, since I had *purposed* that my mouth would not sin, that all I did was transgress? He very lovingly spoke to my heart, *Cynthia, you are not sinning any more with your tongue than you have in the past; you are just more aware of it now.* Bernard of Clairvaux confirmed my experience, "Our sense of sin is in proportion to our nearness to God." A good indication that I am traveling on the highway of holiness, then, is my acute sensitivity to sin and my desire to deal with it.

===

*"How would you characterize your
sensitivity to your own sin?"*

===

Frederick Temple provides encouragement for our part in seeking God's holiness when the world outside us and the impulses inside us seem to work against our efforts:

> If any man compares his own soul with the picture drawn in the New Testament of what a Christian ought to be; if any man fixes his eye on the pattern of self-sacrifice, of purity, of truth, of tenderness, and measures his own distance from that standard, he might be ready to despair. But fear not, because you are far from being like the pattern set before you, fear not because your faults are painful to think of, continue the battle and fear not. If, indeed, you

are content with yourself, and are making no endeavor to rise above the poor level at which you now stand, then there is reason to fear. But if you are fighting with all your might, fear not, however often you may have fallen, however deeply, however ungratefully, however inexcusably.[5]

Clothes play a major part in any trip. Taking care of your clothes is important, and the need will continue throughout your lifetime. In your spiritual journey, it is necessary to understand how to read the "climate" and put on the proper clothing. "Buy your clothes from me," the Lord invited the church in Laodicea, "clothes designed in Heaven" (Rev. 3:17 *The Message*).

You travel on the highway of holiness, and you must be dressed appropriately. It's a daily process to make sure your clothes are clean. But you may take comfort on this journey in the reality that you always know what to wear! God has told us what pleases Him. Righteous clothing accompanied by a bright, burning torch makes a great-looking outfit for the journey to the heart of God.

> *My Jesus, I love Thee,*
> *I know Thou art mine;*
> *For Thee all the follies of sin I resign;*
> *My gracious Redeemer, my Savior art Thou:*
> *If ever I loved Thee, my Jesus, 'tis now.*[6]

Wise
Traveling
Companions

**When we are pulled to that which is lovely and
Christlike, when we notice someone who is living
a radically obedient life, then those are the best
impulses to act on. This is when it is definitely
worth taking a risk in reaching out to someone.
For we will become like our closest friends.**

Dee Brestin[1]

Nothing makes a trip more enjoyable than easygoing, reliable traveling companions. I have been with a group of people in a caravan, and we have *all* gotten lost! I have traveled with people who were not discreet with their conversation. On one tour there was a dear person who was always late getting on the bus. Another time there was a couple who continually complained about the food, beds, and weather. Nothing can spoil a trip more than fellow travelers who fail to exercise sound judgment. It is always a good idea to travel with discerning, like-hearted friends.

A Friend
for the Road

"I have just had the experience of a lifetime. An angel has appeared to me! Whom can I talk to? Who will believe me? Who will understand? Whom can I pray with? Why, Elizabeth! She is perfect. She is pregnant as well, and her husband was visited by an angel who announced the event. Yes, Elizabeth. I'll hurry to be with her."

Mary needed companionship after the revelation that she had been chosen to bear the Messiah. She needed another woman who could share her astonishing news—someone who was wise, who would listen, and who would provide encouragement and support. Few of us have visits with Gabriel to talk about, but the principle of having godly relationships on our journey is just as vital for us as it was for Mary. Whether we have sorrowful or joyful news, our burdens can be eased and our joy increased by sharing it with a good friend—one we can trust to respond caringly and wisely.

> *We will not always be able to travel with living wise friends, but we are surrounded by a wonderful "cloud of witnesses" who have traveled this road ahead of us.*

On our journey in life, we have many and varied relationships. But in considering the essentials we need along the way, I want to concentrate on the importance of walking with *wise* friends. Friends with sound judgment are invaluable in supporting and guiding us as we travel. The writer of Proverbs affirms, "Whoever walks with the wise will become wise; whoever walks with fools will suffer harm" (Prov. 13:20 NLT).

What Will She Look Like?

One of your first questions may be, "How will I know a wise person when I see one?" Paul's advice to Timothy provided an important clue: "Pursue faith and love and peace, and enjoy the companionship of those who call on the Lord with pure hearts" (2 Tim. 2:22 NLT).

Dee Brestin's counsel to look for someone who is "lovely and Christlike" and lives "a radically obedient life" is a good description of a wise woman. Any woman who has these qualities is a woman who fears the Lord, which is the beginning of wisdom. She will communicate a sense of authenticity and honesty in her life.

When you notice a woman with these qualities and you begin to interact with her, it should be apparent that she uses the Word of God and prayer as a basis for her decisions and in her relationships with others. She is certainly not perfect, but whenever you are around her, you will see indications that her journey is toward the heart of God.

James sketches a profile of the qualities of wisdom: "The wisdom that comes from heaven is first of all pure. It is also peace loving, gentle at all times, and willing to yield to others. It is full of mercy and good deeds. It shows no partiality and is always sincere" (James 3:17 NLT).

"What is your definition of a wise traveling companion?"

Where Can I Find Such a Friend?

Your next question may be, "How in the world am I ever going to be able to find a woman like this?" I'm guessing that you may be thinking, *I've met only one woman who came close to these qualities—and she's now a full-time missionary in Santiago, Chile!* Good point, but let's see how God provides for us.

I've enjoyed the story Eugene Peterson tells of a young man who was exploited by religious leaders and, in frustration and disillusionment, fled to the world of drugs. While in Mexico, he met some former drug dealers who had recently become Christians. They witnessed to him and prayed for him, and he went back home with a desire to renew his faith. "One day he went into a bookstore and asked the manager, 'Do you have any books by dead Christians? I don't trust anybody living.'"[2]

We will not always be able to travel with *living* wise friends, but we are surrounded by a wonderful "cloud of witnesses" who have traveled this road ahead of us. Many of them have taken the time to record their experiences and insights on the path of faith. We have a wealth of wisdom, therefore, from godly men and women who can counsel and guide us as we listen to them speak through their writings. I consider many of these "old" saints my good, wise friends.

Of course, it is not necessary to be deceased in order to qualify as a wise author! Perhaps your missionary friend in Chile writes books or letters. You can benefit from people who are alive today through their books, speaking, and letter writing. There is much wisdom to be mined in articles, tapes, and seminars. My point is that you may not have a personal, one-on-one relationship with a wise friend, but you will find that wisdom is available for those who seek it.

Face-to-Face Relationships

Of course, the very best relationship is a personal, life-to-life, enduring relationship. For this blessing, you pray. As I have prayed for older women, for friends my age, and for younger women to relate to, God has been faithful to provide. Keep in mind these two suggestions: (1) *don't be in a hurry,* and (2) *don't discount anyone.* I have often been surprised at the individuals God placed before me. Once I prayed for someone with whom I could have an accountable relationship, and the Lord brought two acquaintances to mind. I would never have thought of them, but their friendship has been a blessing to my life.

> *Simple companionship is a wonderful and necessary part of our lives, but a good, wise friend meets us at our point of need and encourages us in the Lord.*

The writer of Ecclesiastes drives home the importance of finding wise friends to accompany us on our journey: "If one person falls, the other can reach out and help. But people who are alone when they fall are in real trouble" (4:10 NLT). This principle of traveling together is exemplified in Jesus' practice of sending out the disciples two by two. We need the strong fellowship of other believers to guide us through the challenges, joys, and uncertainties of the territory ahead.

❦

Simple companionship is a wonderful and necessary part of our lives, but a good, wise friend meets us at our point of need and encourages us in the Lord. This ability to strengthen our faith makes *wise* friends indispensable. David and Jonathan provide a prime example: "One day near Horesh, David received the news that Saul was on the way to Ziph to search for him and kill him. Jonathan went to find David and encouraged him to stay strong in his faith in God" (1 Sam. 23:15–16 NLT).

Wise friends differ from other kinds of relationships in their desire to increase our faith. It is indeed rare to find this kind of friend, and physical proximity is not always possible. Two friends I rely on for wisdom live in other states, but I phone when I am seeking counsel. Whatever it takes to have someone you can call or write, it is worth the effort. We may go through seasons when we do not have a Jonathan to be there for us in our time of need. But we always have a Friend who is with us to provide comfort, to speak to us through the Scriptures, and to support us through the godly writings of others who testify to His sufficiency.

―――

"What opportunities do you have to be
a wise friend to another?"

―――

A Friend's Godly Influence

The more we grow to prize the gift of godly friends, the more receptive we will be to their influence in our lives.

A wise friend will set the pace for you in your journey on the highway of holiness: "But encourage one another day after day, as long as it is still called 'Today,' lest any one of you be hardened by the deceitfulness of sin" (Heb. 3:13 NASB). A friend's "daily" presence can mean that she walks with you through the changing seasons of your life, regardless of the frequency of your contact, prompting you to follow the Lord in all your circumstances.

By her example of purity as well as her concern for you, a wise friend will make you sensitive to sin and encourage you to keep your heart softened toward God. A godly friend will challenge you to the best and the highest. As I write these words, I think of Oswald Chambers, who, year after year, has exhorted me to give my utmost for His highest. We need such exhortations, and we need to be around those who are concerned about the deceitfulness of sin.

❦

Those who are truly wise and who really love us will encourage us in the Lord and urge us on to purity. The writer of Proverbs said that they will even wound us for our good: "Faithful are the wounds of a friend, / But deceitful are the kisses of an enemy" (Prov. 27:6 NASB).

What kind of wound does a friend inflict? Proverbs 25:12 describes it this way: "Valid criticism is as treasured by the one who heeds it as jewelry made from finest gold" (NLT). I like Laurence Peter's criterion: "You can always tell a real friend: when you've made a fool of yourself, he doesn't feel you've done a permanent job."[3]

I remember one occasion in which I was visiting with numerous people I knew at a social gathering. Later in the evening, our youngest daughter joined us. After she came in and we talked for a minute, she took me aside and told me I had lettuce in my teeth. I could have died! In a way, I felt hurt that no one else seemed to care enough to let me know. A friend is willing to correct us for our benefit.

Another time, I had opportunity to return the favor for someone else. I had just loaded groceries into the car and was driving out of the parking lot when I noticed a woman going into the store whose pants were unzipped. I was already on my way, but I couldn't go on. I parked again, got out, ran into the store, found this dear woman, and let her know. She was so thankful, I felt we could have started a lifelong friendship right then and there.

These are fairly minor examples of criticism, but they help depict the biblical principle that a faithful friend will let you know when something is not right in your life. I have one particular friend I consult when I especially need perspective and counsel. I go to her because I know that she will always speak the truth, even though it might wound me. I hold her in high regard for this quality.

_____

*"How have you been influenced by the
'faithful wounds' of a friend?"*

_____

The Hebrew word for "friend" used by the Proverbs writer in connection with "wounds" carries the meaning to "have affection for." This is important, for any profitable wounding you receive should be from those who have affection for you. Proverbs 12:18 provides a helpful commentary here: "Some people make cutting remarks, but the words of the wise bring healing" (NLT). When the words of a wise traveling companion bring correction, you know in your heart, *Yes, she is right. I'm thankful that she cares enough about me to let me know. This is like jewelry made from the finest gold.*

Not all such correction has to come from personal, face-to-face friends. Writers such as Amy Carmichael have chastened me. Listen to these reproofs from her book *IF*:

IF a sudden jar can cause me to speak an impatient, unloving word, then I know nothing of Calvary love.

IF I can enjoy a joke at the expense of another; if I can in any way slight another in conversation, or even in thought, then I know nothing of Calvary love.

IF I take offense easily, if I am content to continue in a cool unfriendliness, though friendship be possible, then I know nothing of Calvary love.[4]

Danger: Traveling Alone

God created us all to be part of His body. We function together. Fellowship is a precious gift the Lord gives His children. To neglect fellowship or refuse to draw near those who can make our journey all that it should be is to make ourselves vulnerable to compromise. Proverbs 18:1 speaks clearly, "He who separates himself seeks his own desire, / He quarrels against all sound wisdom" (NASB). The New Living Translation says, "A recluse is self-indulgent, snarling at every sound principle of conduct." Jonah was probably a good example of someone who separated himself and sought his own desire. He ran in the opposite direction—away from God, and away from anyone who might try to help him stay on the path.

Anytime we withdraw from wise friends who will hold us accountable, we seek our own desires. We become resistant to "all sound wisdom"—and that is a precarious place to be. If we are committed to travel toward the heart of God, then we need to move toward the wise friends, of any age, who can help us stay on the journey.

"Who are the wise friends in your journey?"

Mary and Elizabeth must have rejoiced again and again as they recounted God's great goodness to them. This companionship made their experiences even more extraordinary. How sweet Elizabeth's words must have been to Mary, for her godly life and wisdom were priceless blessings to Mary at that time. A young woman who had just received such an "assignment" from God needed the comforting words Elizabeth would speak. As they prayed and spoke together, both were strengthened in the Lord. This season of fellowship was vital in preparing and encouraging each of them for the experiences that lay ahead.

Praying for wise friends is key in discerning who these individuals might be in your life. God wants you to have this fellowship and encouragement, so persevere in prayer and be on the alert for whoever might cross your path. Don't be afraid to make the first move toward friendship. As you meet with someone and notice her walk with God, ask if she would be available to you as a source of counsel. Go out of your way to meet a few classic Christian authors, and make sure they take up residence in your library. Spend time with them—through their books they will always be accessible, any time of the day or night. Making wise friends is a wise choice for the journey.

> *Blest be the tie that binds*
> *Our hearts in Christian love;*
> *The fellowship of kindred minds*
> *Is like to that above.*[5]

Willingness to Endure

Jeremiah did not resolve to stick it out for twenty-three years, no matter what; he got up every morning with the sun. The day was God's day, not the people's. He didn't get up to face rejection, he got up to meet with God. He didn't rise to put up with another round of mockery, he rose to be with his Lord. That is the secret of his persevering pilgrimage.

Eugene H. Peterson[1]

S ome tours can be quite rigorous. As I have been sightseeing, sometimes the tour guide would make it clear that it would take a fair amount of strength to climb the stairs or hike the trail to see a certain landmark. Those who felt they could make it followed the guide; those who couldn't stayed behind. Stamina was necessary to see all the sights.

Once our family hiked down the Grand Canyon. Since we were camping for two nights, we hiked with our backpacks full of food and bedding. (There were times along the way when I wondered if I would make it!) After the twelve-mile hike, we all arrived at the campsite with weary muscles and many blisters. But our fortitude was rewarded when, at the bottom of the canyon, we were greeted by the overwhelming beauty of the most incredible waterfall we had ever seen. How richly blessed we were for persevering on our journey!

When the Road Is Rough . . .

. . . And the Path Is Long

Jeremiah was a prophet beginning in 626 B.C. He was called to preach to Judah that their apostasy would lead to their ultimate destruction. As you might imagine, his preaching did not make him a popular figure. He was accused of treason and imprisoned numerous times. On at least one occasion, he was cast into a slimy cistern. Jeremiah tried to convince the Lord that he could not speak, and besides, he was too young! But God reassured him, "Do not be afraid of them, for I am with you to deliver you." In essence, God said, "This is My chosen journey for you. I will give you the words, and I will deliver you. Your part is to trust, be faithful, and persevere."

> *Jeremiah chose endurance because he knew the destination was worth it.*

And persevere he did. Listen to Jeremiah's prayer of dependence on the Lord's words:

> Thou who knowest, O LORD,
> Remember me, take notice of me,
> And take vengeance for me on my persecutors.
> Do not, in view of Thy patience, take me away;
> Know that for Thy sake I endure reproach. (Jer. 15:15 NASB)

> Your words are what sustain me. They bring me great joy
> and are my heart's delight, for I bear your name, O LORD God
> Almighty. (Jer. 15:16 NLT)

I like Jeremiah's honesty with God. He complained:

> O LORD, you persuaded me, and I allowed myself to be per-
> suaded. You are stronger than I am, and you overpowered me.

Now I am mocked by everyone in the city. Whenever I speak, the words come out in a violent outburst. "Violence and destruction!" I shout. So these messages from the LORD have made me a household joke. And I can't stop! If I say I'll never mention the LORD or speak in his name, his word burns in my heart like a fire. . . . But the LORD stands beside me like a great warrior. Before him they will stumble. They cannot defeat me. They will be shamed and thoroughly humiliated . . . for I have committed my cause to you. (Jer. 20:7–9, 11–12 NLT)

Jeremiah's journey was filled with continual rejection, deprivation, and loneliness. He was single and had few friends. How was he able to endure? As Peterson says, Jeremiah woke up each day and greeted it as a day *with* and *for* the Lord. He declared that the Lord was his great warrior (the New American Standard Bible translation renders it "dread champion"). God's words sustained him daily; he committed himself to the Lord and affirmed that commitment each day; and he knew that he was on the winning side.

> *I think God prompts each of us to a decisive moment in which we surrender to His purposes.*

Jeremiah chose endurance because he knew the destination was worth it. He had a very long history of obedience in the same direction—constant perseverance characterized his whole life.

Sometimes, however, the decision to be steadfast must be exercised quickly.

. . . And the Heat Is Intense

The king was extremely angry. He exploded into a fit of rage. He had built a gold statue, ninety feet tall and nine feet wide. It was beautiful, and it was his statue. He had ordered everyone to bow down and worship it whenever the musicians played. Refusal to bow down meant instant death in the fiery furnace. Now he had just received word that Shadrach, Meshach, and Abednego were in defiance of his command.

The king ordered the three rebels to be brought before him immediately. He went so far as to give them one more chance to bow down.

He taunted them with these threats: "But if you refuse, you will be thrown immediately into the blazing furnace. What god will be able to rescue you from my power then?"

Shadrach, Meshach, and Abednego replied,

> O Nebuchadnezzar, we do not need to defend ourselves before you. If we are thrown into the blazing furnace, the God whom we serve is able to save us. He will rescue us from your power, Your Majesty. But even if he doesn't, Your Majesty can be sure that we will never serve your gods or worship the gold statue you have set up. (Dan. 3:15–18 NLT)

What an incredible illustration of a commitment to stand firm! "Whatever our God has for us on this journey we will accept—His deliverance or death, but we will never forsake Him or worship any other God."

Gary Inrig points out:

> The word *endure* comes from two Greek words that combine to say, "to remain under." Endurance is that capacity to stay under the load, to remain in the circumstances, without fleeing or seeking the easy way out. . . . There is one other thing we should notice about the word *endure*. It is not primarily a negative or passive quality. It does not mean that we submit ourselves to difficult circumstances with a spirit of resignation and defeat. The idea behind the word is that of a soldier staying in the heat of the battle, under terrible opposition but pressing forward to gain a victory.[2]

Certainly, Jeremiah represented a soldier under attack who chose to stay in the heat of battle rather than flee. Shadrach, Meshach, and Abednego were steadfast in their willingness to endure the heat of the furnace even unto certain death.

Perseverance is a quality we must exercise on a daily basis. But to be prepared to endure whatever comes our way, we need to lay a foundational commitment. I think God prompts each of us to a decisive moment in which we surrender to His purposes and declare, "Lord, my life is Yours, and I will be steadfast and continue on my journey to Your heart, no matter what

I may encounter." This affirmation can be an important predecision that is essential to have in place when we find ourselves in the midst of a crisis. We never know when we might be thrown into a fiery furnace. Job went so far as to declare, "Though He slay me, / I will hope in Him" (Job 13:15 NASB). Jeremiah knew the course of his life, and he set his heart to continue on it each day. Shadrach, Meshach, and Abednego were steadfast in their walk with

What we consider affliction, the Lord uses to manifest His strength in us.

God. When the time of testing arrived, there was no debate about whom they would worship.

"Can you say this to God right now? 'Lord, my life is Yours. I will be steadfast and continue on my journey to Your heart, no matter what I may encounter.'"

. . . And God Is Applying the Pressure

The apostle Paul's life is a model of endurance. Like Jeremiah, Paul knew that he had been called to suffer. But in my opinion, the unique part of Paul's journey was his thorn in the flesh. As if Paul did not have enough hardship to contend with, the Lord sent a "thorn" in his flesh. We are not told what it was, but we do know it was extremely irritating. Three times, Paul prayed for it to be removed.

God had applied that pressure in Paul's life to keep him from being prideful, but along with the affliction God supplied Paul with the grace to endure:

At first I didn't think of it as a gift, and begged God to remove it. Three times I did that, and then he told me,

"My grace is enough; it's all you need. My strength comes into its own in your weakness."

Once I heard that, I was glad to let it happen. I quit focusing on the handicap and began appreciating the gift. It was a case of

Christ's strength moving in on my weakness. (2 Cor. 12:8–10 *The Message*)

When God places us in difficult situations and declines to eliminate the pressure, it is comforting to remember that His grace enables us to keep going when the road is rough. What we consider affliction, the Lord uses to manifest His strength in us. James tells us, "For when your faith is tested, your endurance has a chance to grow. So let it grow, for when your endurance is fully developed, you will be strong in character and ready for anything" (James 1:3–4 NLT). Scripture permits us to witness the results: Jeremiah's character grew strong as iron, and Paul became ready for anything.

"How is God cultivating endurance in your life right now?"

We will have many opportunities for growth in our endurance, and we need to embrace all of them. There may be times, however, when we encounter unexpected roadblocks, and endurance requires us to take the initiative and do the *acting* rather than the *reacting*. In these cases, God's grace becomes evident almost after the fact. Scripture provides an example in a portrait of a woman who suddenly found herself up against seemingly impossible odds, requiring her to act quickly and creatively.

. . . And the Odds Seem Impossible

The troublemaker Sheba decided to rebel against King David. He ran off to rally his own people. Joab, David's commander, pursued him to the city of Abel. Joab built a ramp against the town wall and began to batter it down. If it meant destroying the entire city to seize the rebel, he would do so.

Scripture tells us there was a "wise woman" dwelling in Abel who took action. She called over the wall to Joab and asked why he was attacking them. "It's really not your city I'm after," Joab explained, "I just need to capture Sheba."

The wise woman wasted no time in replying.

"All right," she said. "We will throw his head over the wall to you."

She ducked back behind the wall to share her plan with her town's inhabitants. Apparently, there was immediate agreement because the next thing that happened was that the residents of Abel cut off Sheba's head and threw it out to Joab (2 Sam. 20:21–22).

I love this story. Here is one wise traveling companion we need to get to know! This dear woman was confronted with a sudden and deadly crisis. How was she going to persevere through it? Should she find the best hiding place possible and simply wait for her city to be destroyed? Should she hope that someone would have the courage to go out there and confront the Hebrew commander? Or should *she* do something?

> *Other times, we must confront what we encounter on our journey with the courage to seize the moment and do battle.*

This woman was, indeed, facing a battle. She was not willing to go down to defeat or to accept the circumstances with a sigh of resignation. She pressed forward to gain a victory if possible. She used her wisdom to fight an enemy. She summoned courage and determination to work through her crisis.

I see this woman as an example of the "creative, courageous" view of enduring. Sometimes, we are called to accept and endure unforeseen circumstances with steadfastness and God's grace. Other times, we must confront what we encounter on our journey with the courage to seize the moment and do battle. In these cases, our endurance is manifested in active vigilance.

I think of the countless, courageous women who have battled cancer. I think of mothers who have fought for their children's lives. Godly, sensitive women have started ministries and initiated serving others because of their commitment to stand firm for what is right and for what is good. When something begins to batter their city, they take action and persevere with the Lord as their "dread champion."

Setting Our Sights

The knowledge that others have persevered before us helps us to be steadfast. Hebrews 11 lists many men and women of faith who endured severe trials. Some were tortured; some were chained in dungeons; some were killed with the sword or sawed in half. Their faith held them so that they could endure until the end.

A fellow believer who has helped to strengthen my endurance is Amy Carmichael, the beloved missionary in India who endured misunderstanding, threats to her safety, and injury and pain for years before she died. She wrote,

> "The only thing that matters is to please Me," that was the word that woke me a few days ago, and it has not gone away. . . . The word—that simple word—reminded me of those other words, "All that pleases is but for a moment. All that grieves is but for a moment. Only the eternal is important." . . . Are any of you tried about anything? I think if you listen you will hear Him say, "The only thing that matters is to please Me."[3]

The great desire of Amy Carmichael's life was to please the Lord in all things. That was Jeremiah's desire as well: "Know that for Thy sake I bear reproach." And why else would Shadrach, Meshach, and Abednego be willing to enter the furnace apart from their desire to honor God? Paul wrote, "Obviously, I'm not trying to be a people pleaser! No, I am trying to please God. If I were still trying to please people, I would not be Christ's servant" (Gal. 1:10 NLT). The honorable men and women listed in the hall of faith were steadfast because they loved God and wanted to bring Him glory through their endurance. We are told that all those people received God's approval because of their faith (Heb. 11:39).

> *The honorable men and women listed in the hall of faith were steadfast because they loved God and wanted to bring Him glory through their endurance.*

When we set our sights on pleasing God, what may we expect to be the outcome of our endurance? Let's look at those who have gone before us: Jeremiah was vindicated, and he saw God deliver him time after time. Shadrach, Meshach, and Abednego lived to see King Nebuchadnezzar praise God and decree that no one could speak against Him. Paul received the assurance that he had earned a crown of righteousness for his endurance.

The wise woman of Abel saved a city. The martyrs who endured deadly persecution gained God's approval. They were able to endure because, in Paul's words, the source of their strength was "the God who gives perseverance and encouragement" (Rom. 15:5 NASB).

"Are you setting your sights on pleasing God
in every difficult situation you face?"

Scripture assures us that endurance has its own reward: "God blesses the people who patiently endure testing. Afterward they will receive the crown of life that God has promised to those who love him" (James 1:12 NLT). And Scripture sets before us the ultimate example of endurance in our Lord: "For consider Him who has endured such hostility by sinners against Himself, so that you may not grow weary and lose heart" (Heb. 12:3 NASB).

I endure because I get up each day to walk with God. I endure because I love God and I want my life to please Him. I know that every trial in which I stand firm will add to my maturity. I know that it will deepen my ability to accept and handle whatever I encounter in life. His Word sustains me; He stands beside me; His grace is sufficient; He *gives* perseverance and encouragement. I want the whole tour; I don't want to miss out on anything the Lord wants me to see or do.

Will you commit with me to "press on" toward His heart and finish your pilgrimage with your torch burning? It is the only journey in which we do not have to endure alone.

> *When through fiery trials thy pathway shall lie,*
> *My grace, all sufficient, shall be thy supply;*
> *The flame shall not hurt thee; I only design*
> *Thy dross to consume and thy gold to refine.*[4]

The Destination: God's Heart

With unfailing love you will lead this
people whom you have ransomed.
You will guide them in your strength
to the place where your holiness
dwells.

Exodus 15:13 NLT

THE FATHER
AND THE CHILD

The child spoke:

*Father, the journey is harder than I thought it would
be. I am weary.*

When My Son traveled here, He became weary
also.

Why is it so?

Because My kingdom is not yet established.

Am I nearing the destination?

You have come far, but there are still many roads
to travel.

Will these roads be any easier?

The closer you come to My heart, the more
intensely you will experience My love and understand My ways. You will become more concerned
about what is eternal and less concerned about
the difficulty of the journey.

Sorrow still walks with me.

She travels with you by My design. She is a carefully chosen tool in My hand to accomplish My
will for you.

*Sorrow has become more of a friend. I no longer fear
her presence. But Joy never leaves me! She has settled
deep within me. Will she always accompany me?*

She will never leave you as long as you keep your
hand in Mine and let Me lead you to My heart.

*Then she will be with me forever—for I have no other
desire than to know Your heart.*

THIRTEEN

His Immeasurable Love

If nothing in us can win Thy love, nothing in the
universe can prevent Thee from loving us. . . .
Help us to believe the intensity, the eternity of
the love that has found us. Then love will cast
out fear; and our troubled hearts will be at peace,
trusting not in what we are but in what Thou
hast declared Thyself to be.

A. W. Tozer[1]

L ooking for love in all the wrong places," laments the refrain of a familiar song. We are all, in one way or another, looking for love. We are willing to take any tour, sign up for any adventure, that might promise us love. We are created to be loved, and our search for love begins early. We travel roads that seem to offer fulfillment, but often at great expense we return wounded. I met a woman who had been married five times. She was tired of looking in all the wrong places. Then she heard of a "place" that bestows a special kind of love on anyone who is willing to receive it. It sounded too good to be true. Love offered freely with no strings attached? How do I get there? When can I go? Show me the brochure!

Can there be any greater incentive to travel to a destination than the guarantee that when we get there, we will experience complete, unconditional, and eternal love? This love is authentic and constant, there are no strings, you can go any time, and you get there by going to the cross. There can be no greater journey than the one to God's heart, for there we are embraced by His immeasurable love.

God-Given Love

There is a passage in Deuteronomy that I find particularly touching: "The LORD did not choose you and lavish his love on you because you were larger or greater than other nations, for you were the smallest of all nations! It was simply because the LORD loves you" (Deut. 7:7–8 NLT). God chose the Israelites for no other reason than because He loved them. They had no special characteristics that would particularly catch God's attention. They were not in any way distinctive from or better than the other nations. He simply chose to lavish His love on them.

> *Can there be any greater incentive to travel to a destination than the guarantee that when we get there, we will experience complete, unconditional, and eternal love?*

For the same reason, God loves us. It has nothing to do with whether we are attractive or lovable; He simply *chooses* to love us. As we grasp the unconditional and utterly free gift of His love, we can begin to rest in that love. Since we can do nothing to captivate His love, we can do nothing to lose it. How critical it is for us to understand this one-of-a-kind, only-God-given love.

Years ago an advice columnist surveyed her readers with the question, "If you had a choice, would you have children again?" Remarkably, 70 percent of the people who responded said they would *not* choose to have children the second time around. Why? Although these "gifts from the Lord" can bring much joy, many children cause their parents pain and heartache.

Listen to what the Lord has experienced from His children:

> "The children I raised and cared for have turned against me. Even the animals—the donkey and the ox—know their owner and

appreciate his care, but not my people Israel. No matter what I do for them, they still do not understand." Oh, what a sinful nation they are! They are loaded down with a burden of guilt. They are evil and corrupt children who have turned away from the LORD. They have despised the Holy One of Israel, cutting themselves off from his help. (Isa. 1:2–4 NLT)

I wonder how the Lord would have responded to that survey! Knowing us, and knowing all the risks in parenting, God still initiates, adopts, and draws us to Himself. To me, this is an incredible, sacrificial, daring kind of love. I think, *God doesn't* need *us! We hurt Him. We rebel. We look for love in all the wrong places. How could He send His own Son to die for us, knowing how independent, ungrateful, and mistrustful we can be?* The only conclusion I can come to is that God is love, and He will do whatever it takes for us to know what Julian of Norwich called His "high, over-passing, immeasurable" love.[2]

The Lord's everlasting love is vividly portrayed in the father who, at his son's request, gave him his inheritance and then watched his son leave home to squander it. The father looked and longed for his son's return, waiting patiently. God's love is not predicated on our actions. His love is constant and continual.

If we refuse to receive His love as the highest privilege of life; if we fail to love Him in return with all our hearts, souls, and minds; then we will journey without the security and freedom that only His love can give.

> *God loves us. It has nothing to do with whether we are attractive or lovable;* *He simply* chooses *to love us.*

On one occasion my husband, Jack, forgot to pick me up at a coffee shop. I was devastated! *How could he forget me?* I thought. *He must not love me! I guess I'm just unlovable!* As I look back on the incident, I realize it taught me a lot. Jack really *does* love me. But he is not perfect, and therefore his love is not perfect. He cannot ever fully meet all my needs, just as I cannot ever fully meet his. There is only One who loves perfectly, and He is the One to whom I must look to be loved completely. Allowing the Lord's love to fulfill the needs of my heart frees me to love others without demanding that they meet my deepest needs. I am able to give love instead of constantly trying to receive love.

"Are you depending on someone other than the Lord to love you in a way that will fulfill your deepest needs?"

That was what happened to the woman at the well. She was desperately seeking love in any relationship she could hold on to. That was why Jesus' statement that she would never have to thirst again was so powerful and life-changing. His salvation could free her from having to spend the rest of her life searching for love.

There is only One who loves perfectly, and He is the One to whom I must look to be loved completely.

In Jesus, we discover the highest and most perfect love—a love we must wholeheartedly receive and embrace as the most precious love in our lives: "If you love your father or mother more than you love me, you are not worthy of being mine; or if you love your son or daughter more than me, you are not worthy of being mine" (Matt. 10:37 NLT). Oswald Chambers described why it is so important to love God above all human loves:

> [If] we love a human being and do not love God, we demand of him every perfection and every rectitude, and when we do not get it we become cruel and vindictive; we are demanding of a human being that which he or she cannot give. There is only one Being Who can satisfy the last aching abyss of the human heart, and that is the Lord Jesus Christ. Why Our Lord is apparently so severe regarding every human relationship is because He knows that every relationship not based on loyalty to Himself will end in disaster.[3]

The great and foremost commandment is, "You shall love the LORD your GOD with all your heart, and with all your soul, and with all your mind." From this "first love," we are able to begin to fulfill the second commandment, "You shall love your neighbor as yourself" (Matt. 22:37–39 NASB). *The order is very important.* Only out of God's love for us are we able to bless and encourage someone else.

How can we fulfill the first and great commandment? My immediate answer is, How can we *not* fulfill this wonderful command to respond to the One whose perfect love has such extravagant dimensions?

Whose Love Is Enough?

Jack and I were attending a large conference, which began with dinner. We sat at one of many round tables and watched as other people came in and were seated. A young single man saw Jack and asked if he could sit down and visit with him during the meal. Eventually, two couples joined our table. The couples were friends but had not seen each other for a while, and they were eager to visit during the meal. That left an empty seat beside me.

We began the meal by introducing ourselves to one another and chatting casually as the meal was served. Once we began eating, the young man immediately engaged Jack's attention, and the couples immersed themselves in earnest conversation. I began to eat alone. As I sat there, by myself, I began to feel very conspicuous. It seemed as if people sitting at the tables around me were whispering to each other, "Isn't it sad? No one wants to sit next to Cynthia or talk to her!" I began to have a lovely pity party. Those attending my private party included "You're no good" and "Nobody loves you."

Then very gently, I heard the Lord's thoughts in my heart, *Cynthia, is it true that no one loves you?*

"Lord, I know You love me," I replied. "But You *have* to love me—I'm Your child!"

The Lord answered, *Yes, Cynthia, I do love you. I love you with an everlasting love. I will never leave you or forsake you. In fact, I'm in this empty chair next to you. But I have a question I must ask: Is My love enough for you?*

It was an extraordinary question, and it forever changed the way I love God and the way I accept His love.

"Yes, Lord, a thousand times, yes," I whispered in my heart. "Your love *is* enough. It doesn't matter if no one talks to me. It doesn't matter if I'm ignored. I don't have to be the center of attention to have my worth affirmed or to know that 'I am my beloved's, / And his desire is for me' [Song 7:10 NASB]. Your love is beyond my comprehension, but it is all I want and all I need. Yes, it is enough for me."

―――――

"Do you believe that God's love is enough for you?"

―――――

If God's love is not enough for us, it has been said, then we are asking too much. I love God for pressing this question on my heart. I love God for not allowing me to wallow in self-pity. I love Him for being such a strong Father that He will not let me get away with trying to live His life on my terms. I love Him for correcting me.

The Discipline of Love

The writer to the Hebrews gave us crucial teaching about God's love:

> "My dear child, don't shrug off God's discipline,
>   but don't be crushed by it either.
> It's the child he loves that he disciplines;
>   the child he embraces, he also corrects."
>
> God is educating you; that's why you must never drop out. He's treating you as dear children. This trouble you're in isn't punishment; it's *training,* the normal experience of children.
> (Heb.12:5–7 *The Message*)

This Scripture is especially important because we don't naturally associate correction with love. What comes naturally is to shun correction as unpleasant, undesirable, and even unnecessary. C. S. Lewis observed,

> We want not so much a father in heaven as a grandfather in heaven, whose plan for the universe was such that it might be said at the end of each day, "A good time was had by all." Oh, I should very much like to live in a universe which was governed on such lines, but since it is abundantly clear that I don't; and since I have

reason to believe, nevertheless, that God is love, I conclude that my conception of love needs correction. The problem of reconciling human suffering with the existence of God who loves is only insoluble so long as we attach a trivial meaning to the word love and limit His wisdom by what seems to us to be wise. How shallow, how foolish to think that a God who truly loves us will never discipline us. That which makes His love authentic is that He does discipline us, and regularly so.[4]

Numbers 12 records a protest that was stirred up against Moses when a few of those close to him began grumbling about his leadership. "I can't believe that my brother married a foreigner. Honestly! And he's supposed to be such an example. Here he is going around like the Lord's anointed, and everyone hanging on his every word. Hasn't the Lord spoken by Aaron and me also? Who does Moses think he is? God's *only* appointed leader?"

Miriam, bless her heart, could no longer contain her jealousy and envy. She and Aaron were in agreement, but she was the ringleader in the minirebellion—her name was listed first. The Lord was angered by their complaints, and He verbally rebuked them both. As a loving Father concerned with what He saw in His child, God disciplined Miriam by exiling her outside the camp with leprosy for an entire week—even over Moses' pleas to heal her.

As I picture this drama, I see the whole nation of Israel sitting around filing their fingernails, jogging, and simply biding their time as they wait on Miriam's "time-out" to be over. I imagine the Lord saying, "Miriam, this desire for recognition, this resentment, is wrong. It hurts you, and it disrupts and causes dissension in My people. I want you to be free of this, and I want you to remember not to do it again."

What a lesson for her! Her rebellion was very public, and so was her discipline. Sometimes we turn away from God when He disciplines us. But He loves us enough to risk His relationship with us so that we might lay aside the sin that can so easily entangle us. It is for our good: "But God's discipline is always right and good for us because it means we will share in his holiness. No discipline is enjoyable while it is happening—it is painful!

But afterward there will be a quiet harvest of right living for those who are trained in this way" (Heb. 12:10–11 NLT).

Perhaps this harvest was realized in Miriam's life. We never hear of her questioning Moses' leadership or his choices again. I think that Miriam was very teachable, and that she had a tender heart for God. She must have been incredibly humbled, but thankful, that God's love is strong and consistent.

When we understand what the Bible teaches about God's discipline, we can draw great security from the assurance that He always chastens in love and always for our best. We can rest in the knowledge that His every word has absolute integrity. Who would not want to share in His holiness and enjoy a journey that consists of living the way He intends for us?

> *On your journey to God's heart, it is critical that you know you are loved.*

Although being struck with leprosy is a fearful thing, I don't believe that Miriam lived in dread of God after her experience. I think she most likely had a marvelous testimony of her respect and reverence for Him. For since God's love is perfect, when His love is properly understood and received, then all anxiety and apprehension disappear. When we accept His love in its totality, we do not live in fear—especially of His discipline and judgment.

"Do you recognize God's correction as evidence of His love for you?"

When We Confuse Love with Feelings

Just as my experience of eating by myself in a crowd led to my feeling "unloved," so it is easy to allow our feelings to dictate our understanding of God's love. Our tendency is to think of discipline as punishment, and punishment as evidence that love is being withheld from us. Before long we are feeling that perhaps God doesn't love us anymore.

I don't think Miriam felt that God had stopped loving her; I think she knew that the chastening proved His love. Indifference ignores our actions; love moves toward us, even in our frailty. I can't count the number of times I told our children, "If I didn't love you, I wouldn't correct you!" After correction and restoration, our love seemed to be stronger. My children gained confidence that I cared about their behavior. Both my correction and my hugs were evidences of my love for them.

―――――

"Do you allow your feelings to dictate
whether or not you trust in God's love for you?"

―――――

C. S. Lewis drew a helpful distinction between love and feelings:

On the whole, God's love for us is a much safer subject to think about than our love for Him. Nobody can always have devout feelings: and even if we could, feelings are not what God principally cares about. Christian Love, either towards God or towards man, is an affair of the will. If we are trying to do His will we are obeying the commandment, "Thou shalt love the Lord thy God." He will give us feelings of love if He pleases. We cannot create them for ourselves, and we must not demand them as a right. But the great thing to remember is that, though our feelings come and go, His love for us does not. It is not wearied by our sins, or our indifference; and, therefore, it is quite relentless in its determination that we shall be cured of those sins, at whatever cost to us, at whatever cost to Him.[5]

On your journey to God's heart, it is critical that you know you are loved. You have the assurance of God that He will never leave you or forsake you (Heb. 13:5). You need never feel "unloved" because His love is everlasting. Your confidence is based in the wonderful truth of that childhood song "Jesus Loves Me, This I Know, for the Bible Tells Me So." He has chosen to love you, and nothing can separate you from His love. His love heals, comforts, and corrects. His love draws you on the journey toward His heart. You may safely cling to Paul's wonderful declaration:

I am convinced that nothing can ever separate us from his love. Death can't, and life can't. The angels can't, and the demons can't. Our fears for today, our worries about tomorrow, and even the powers of hell can't keep God's love away. Whether we are high above the sky or in the deepest ocean, nothing in all creation will ever be able to separate us from the love of God that is revealed in Christ Jesus our Lord. (Rom. 8:38–39 NLT)

Lord, Your immeasurable love is enough for me. Thank You that Your love is not dependent on my performance or my physical characteristics. Your love encompasses all of my life, and this gives me great security. I would not choose any other destination. I know I am looking in the right place for love—Your heart.

I've found a Friend, O such a Friend!
He loved me ere I knew Him;
He drew me with the cords of love,
And thus He bound me to Him.
And 'round my heart still closely twine
Those ties which can't be severed.
For I am His, and He is mine,
Forever and forever.[6]

FOURTEEN

His Boundless Grace

Love that goes upward is worship; love that goes outward is affection; love that stoops is grace.

Donald Barnhouse[1]

Whenever Jack and I travel to a major city, we like to take an around-the-city bus tour. We enjoy getting an overview of the area and learning interesting facts. We have experienced a varied assortment of guides on these circuits. I recall one guide who seemed to regard his group as an annoying intrusion into his life. He was abrupt in his manner and generally seemed to be having a bad day. When a woman asked if he would mind stopping for a minute so she could take a picture of a certain landmark, he replied curtly, "Lady, if I stop for you, I'll have to stop for everybody, and I gotta get home sometime today." In contrast, I have fond memories of a guide who was friendly and considerate to us all. One of his opening statements was, "Now, if you see anything you want me to stop for, just let me know." What a dramatic difference it was to be greeted kindly and made to feel welcome.

The Scriptures teach that one of the chief expressions of God's love is His gracious treatment of us:

Thus he shows for all the ages to come the tremendous generosity of the grace and kindness he has expressed towards us in Christ

Jesus. For it is by grace that you are saved, through faith. This does not depend on anything you have achieved, it is the free gift of God; and because it is not earned no man can boast about it. (Eph. 2:7–9 PHILLIPS)

Grace
That Saves

What is happening? Her heart was beating so fast, she could hardly breathe. She was absolutely terrified. The men were so angry and determined. *What are they saying?* She strained to hear their words.

"We've got Him this time! He said He came to fulfill the law. He can't get out of this one!"

She could barely think, it was all happening so fast. Just a minute ago she had been alone with a man, and then the next thing she knew the intruders were rushing in on them. Now they were roughly pulling her away and dragging her to the temple.

Am I dressed adequately? Where are my sandals? Why are we going to the temple? What will they do to me there?

She heard Him speak the most gracious, blessed words she had ever heard in her life: "Neither do I [condemn you]. Go and sin no more."

They flung her toward a man who was teaching. The Pharisees, very satisfied with their deed, began to accuse her boldly: "Teacher, this woman was caught in the very act of adultery. We witnessed it ourselves! The law says to stone her. What do You say?"

She knew what the law said, and she could already hear this "teacher" say, "The law is always correct. Stone her!"

But the Teacher said nothing. To her amazement, He began to write in the dust.

The men kept demanding an answer. She felt faint, humiliated, scared, and alone. She knew she was going to die.

Finally, the Teacher stood up, looked piercingly into their eyes, and said, "All right, stone her."

Her heart stopped, and she began to shake.

Then the Teacher added, "But let those who have never sinned throw the first stones."

After He spoke, there was a long, awkward silence. The Teacher bent down and began to write in the dust again.

Very slowly, with resignation, her accusers left one by one. She was stunned; she could not move.

Then the Teacher asked her, "Where are your accusers? Didn't even one of them condemn you?"

Her mouth was dry; she could only whisper, "No, Lord." *Can it be true? Are they no longer denouncing me? Have the men really left? Am I going to live?* As she looked at the Teacher, she felt safe and, in an incredibly strange way, pure.

And then she heard Him speak the most gracious, blessed words she had ever heard in her life: "Neither do I. Go and sin no more." (See John 8:1–11.)

🍂

Grace: mercy, forgiveness, compassion, blessing, love, kindness—all personified in our Lord. Our God is boundless in grace. Before Him, we are all like the woman caught in adultery; we have all sinned. We stand accused.

But God does not condemn us to death under the law. He extends His unmerited, special favor to us. His grace is even more precious because it is free to us, but supremely costly to Him. God Himself paid the price so that He could freely lavish His grace upon us:

> God is so rich in mercy, and he loved us so very much, that even while we were dead because of our sins, he gave us life when he raised Christ from the dead. (It is only by God's special favor that you have been saved!) For he raised us from the dead along with Christ, and we are seated with him in the heavenly realms—all because we are one with Christ Jesus. (Eph. 2:4–6 NLT)

The hymnist voices my response to such saving grace:

> And can it be that I should gain
> An interest in the Savior's blood?
> Died He for me, who caused His pain?
> For me, who Him to death pursued?

Amazing love! how can it be
That Thou, my God, shouldst die for me?[2]

Such amazing love and amazing grace are beyond our understanding—
we can accept them only with deep humility and a profound thankful-
ness.

———

"How are you experiencing God's grace in your life?"

———

Grace
That Pardons

I am always moved by the Lord's grace bestowed upon the woman taken
in adultery, but I tend to get a little annoyed when I read about how God
was gracious to Manasseh, a corrupt king of Judah. There were so many
reasons for God to punish him without hope of pardon:

He was boldly idolatrous. He rebuilt the hills on which Canaanite religious shrines were mounted, reerected altars to Baal, and even made
Asherah poles—pagan symbols of fertility—which he defiantly placed
along with other pagan altars in the temple
courtyards and the very temple itself. He also
brought back Assyrian astral worship and paid
homage to the "heavenly" gods.

> **This is God's
> unmerited favor in
> living color.**

He encouraged immorality. His promotion
of idolatry led to licentiousness and sexual
degradation among the Hebrew nation.

He practiced human sacrifice. Manasseh went so far in his debauch-
ery as to offer his own sons to the Ammonite god Molech.

He promoted sorcery, divination, mediums, and spiritists. In flagrant vio-
lation of the Mosaic Law, Manasseh indulged in a profusion of forbidden
practices in attempts to predict the future and gain control over people
and events.

He destroyed the Word of God. Manasseh was so thorough in burning
the sacred scrolls that it was major news during his grandson's reign when

a copy of the Book of the Law was found while the temple was undergoing renovation.

He murdered his own people. Many of the Judeans were killed because they resisted Manasseh's policy of idolatry. Jerusalem was filled with innocent blood.

He was the likely executioner of the prophet Isaiah. Scholars generally attribute Isaiah's death to Manasseh. According to Jewish tradition, Manasseh had him sawed in two.

> *The more we learn to receive and depend upon His grace in deepening measure, the less anxious we will be about what the future holds.*

Because of Manasseh's overwhelming wickedness, God brought a strong judgment upon Judah. Assyria captured Jerusalem in the twenty-third year of Manasseh's reign, and he was taken prisoner. They put a hook through his nose, bound him with bronze chains, and took him to Babylon.

At this point I am cheering on the punishment. *Yes, God! I can't think of anyone more deserving of suffering than this man. After all he has done to offend You, to lead others astray, and to cause so much pain, he needs to be punished severely. A nose hook and chains are perfect for him, and I know that Assyria's prisons offer no comfort. You made a good choice!*

Now listen to the Scriptures:

> But while in deep distress, Manasseh sought the LORD his God and cried out humbly to the God of his ancestors. And when he prayed, the LORD listened to him and was moved by his request for help. So the LORD let Manasseh return to Jerusalem and to his kingdom. Manasseh had finally realized that the LORD alone is God! (2 Chron. 33:12–13 NLT)

This is God's unmerited favor in living color. Manasseh's sins were a vile abomination to the Lord. If it were up to me, I would have left him to die in prison. Yet when Manasseh repented, God extended him grace.

Manasseh could sing with John Newton, indeed with us all, of "amazing grace . . . that saved a wretch like me." God's grace knows no bounds. It is not dispensed according to our performance, good or bad, but it is given as a free gift to those who believe "that the LORD alone is God."

Grace That Is Sufficient

In an earlier chapter on endurance, we looked at how God declined to remove Paul's thorn in the flesh and in the process developed in him the ability to persevere on a difficult journey:

> So tremendous, however, were the revelations that God gave me that, in order to prevent my becoming absurdly conceited, I was given a stabbing pain—one of Satan's angels—to plague me and effectually stop any conceit. Three times I begged the Lord for it to leave me, but his reply has been, "My grace is enough for you: for where there is weakness, my power is shown the more completely." (2 Cor. 12:7–9 PHILLIPS)

Our *willingness* to endure is an essential that we bring to our journey—but the *ability* to endure is a gift from the Lord. The more we learn to receive and depend upon His grace in deepening measure, the less anxious we will be about what the future holds and whether we will have the strength to face it. Our journey to the Father's heart will intensify our confidence in His grace to infuse strength in the midst of suffering. That was the basis for Paul's proclamation, "For I can do everything with the help of Christ who gives me the strength I need" (Phil. 4:13 NLT). It doesn't matter what we encounter in life, what we must endure, what burdens we bear—God's grace is sufficient to carry us through.

I think of a dear woman I met with several years ago at a church conference. We had met some four years earlier, also at a church retreat. During our first meeting, we enjoyed a lively conversation and began corresponding with each other. In the years between my two visits, she contracted cancer. Now, at my second visit, she was eager to meet with me again and fill me in on how she was doing.

This friend had lost all of her hair from the chemotherapy treatment she was undergoing. She was at the conference for only a day because she had to get back that evening to attend to the needs of her son, who was living in her home. He was in his forties at the time. He had sustained irreparable brain damage in a car accident, and he was dying. She was caring for him at the same time that she was fighting the cancer.

One of the reasons she wanted to see me, she said, was to tell me that she was not discouraged because she had such a strong sense of God's presence with her. I will never forget this woman's face as she spoke with me that day. Her countenance was radiant as she testified to God's grace for her through her experiences. Our encounter was one of those instances when instead of giving encouragement, as I had been expecting, I found myself receiving it.

We know we are nearing the Father's heart when we discover the boundless sufficiency of His grace in those difficult places where we might least expect it. Scripture recounts a litany of the Lord's faithfulness to supply grace according to our need:

- God's grace was sufficient for Hagar when the Lord asked her to return to Sarai, her harsh mistress who manipulated events to ensure Hagar's pregnancy and then resented her for it.
- God's grace was sufficient for Ruth, who seemed headed for a dead-end life when she went to Bethlehem with Naomi to glean in the fields.
- God's grace was sufficient for Joseph when he was a slave, a prisoner, and a prime minister.
- God's grace was sufficient for David when Saul was in constant, deadly pursuit of him.
- God's grace was sufficient for Daniel in the lions' den.
- God's grace was sufficient for Peter when he denied Christ.
- God's grace was sufficient for Paul to fight the good fight and to finish the race.
- God's grace is sufficient for you, no matter what you are going through.

I don't know how many times in my life I have said, "Lord, I can't do this." Each time the Lord has patiently replied, *I know you can't, Cynthia. But I can through you.* And that is the mystery and the good news of the sufficiency of His grace in our lives. And it is the comfort of knowing that

God delights in working through those who are weak, inadequate, and unworthy. For His strength is made perfect in our weakness, His Spirit is our adequacy, and Christ in us makes us worthy.

Paul gave Timothy the admonition, "You therefore, my son, be strong in the grace that is in Christ Jesus" (2 Tim. 2:1 NASB). Our strength is in His grace and His grace alone. It is not in our abilities, in our accomplishments past or present, in our successful service, or in our praise and emulation of others. To be strong in His grace, we must learn to take hold of it and appropriate it for our needs.

Hebrews 4:15–16 teaches us how to take hold of God's grace with this encouragement: "This High Priest of ours understands our weaknesses, for he faced all of the same temptations we do, yet he did not sin. So let us come boldly to the throne of our gracious God. There we will receive his mercy, and we will find grace to help us when we need it" (NLT).

To be strong in His grace, *we must come to the throne of grace*. When Paul agonized over his thorn, he didn't go off in a corner to complain. He went to the Lord with his need and prayed for the thorn to be removed.

═══

"How do you draw upon the Lord for
His gracious strength?"

═══

Scripture tells us that when we come to the throne of grace, acknowledging our need, we will receive God's grace and mercy (Heb. 4:15–16). I experienced this promise during the period in which my dad was dying, and I was flying back and forth to be with my parents while still trying to be with Jack and maintain my speaking schedule. My mom was worn out from taking care of my dad, and so I would stay with them as long and as often as I could. The press of the circumstances drove me frequently to the throne of grace, where I regularly received His strength in my weakness.

Acts 20:32 imparts specific instruction for how to appropriate God's strength in our times of need: "And now I entrust you to God and the word of his grace—his message that is able to build you up and give you an inheritance with all those he has set apart for himself" (NLT).

To be strong in His grace, *we must abide in the Word of His grace.* His Word can build us up and give us strength. During a period in which I was struggling through a trial, I drew great strength from Romans 12:1. The New Living Translation renders it, "And so, dear Christian friends, I plead with you to give your bodies to God. Let them be a living and holy sacrifice—the kind he will accept. When you think of what he has done for you, is this too much to ask?"

> *To view our trials as a means of experiencing more deeply the power of Christ is to understand that God is enough.*

The trial involved a writing project that placed unusual pressures on me. Writing is generally not an easy process for me anyway; the words come only with much effort and prayer. During that period, one of the hardest things I did was to put my body in front of the computer each day. As this verse permeated my heart, I realized that I needed to present my body first as a daily offering. When I placed my body where it should be, to be used by the Lord, then I began to experience His strength. If my body was not where it was supposed to be, then it was hard for God to encourage me.

This verse applies to every area of our lives—raising children, taking care of elderly parents, enduring a challenging work situation, suffering illness. Placing our bodies in obedience to the circumstances God has given us enables us to receive His grace. His gracious Word taught me that, and it has made all the difference in my perseverance.

After Paul described the sufficiency of God's grace in His refusal to grant Paul's request to take away his problem, he continued, "Therefore, I have cheerfully made up my mind to be proud of my weaknesses, because they mean a deeper experience of the power of Christ. I can even enjoy weaknesses, insults, privations, persecutions and difficulties for Christ's sake. For my very weakness makes me strong in him" (2 Cor. 12:10 PHILLIPS).

These are strong words—grace empowers us to meet persecutions and difficulties with joy. I am reminded of an account of the early church martyrs:

> The faithful, while they were dragged along, proceeded with
> cheerful steps; their countenances shone with much grace and

glory; their bonds were as the most beautiful ornaments; and they themselves looked as brides adorned with their richest array, breathing the fragrance of Christ. They were put to death in various ways: or, in other words, they wove a chaplet of various odours and flowers, and presented it to the Father.[3]

To view our trials as a means of experiencing more deeply the power of Christ is to understand that God is enough. Certainly, it was the strength of His grace those martyrs appropriated as they went to their deaths. Their faces shone with His grace and glory. They were given supernatural strength to endure. And so it is with us—no matter what we encounter, we can come to the throne and receive grace from His boundless supply.

Grace That We Extend to Others

In my years of driving, I have made a few miscalculated turns in front of other cars. In each case, I thought I had been using good judgment until the moment I made the turn and suddenly realized that I hadn't allowed enough time. Some drivers would honk (and they were justified in doing so!). One time a man was so angry at me that he pulled around me and deliberately cut back in front of me so closely that he narrowly missed hitting my car. (By now you're probably making a mental note never to ride in a car with me.) I'll never forget the man I pulled in front of who drove up alongside me, got my attention, and then smiled and waved as if to say, "It's okay; I've done it too." Even though I was in the wrong and could have caused an accident, the person I offended said by his actions, "I am not angry. You don't need to feel foolish or ashamed." When we make allowance for others' faults, we extend grace to them, and I was reminded that day that it is an absolute blessing to receive it.

Paul's instruction to the Ephesians clearly indicates that we are to be givers as well as receivers of God's grace, one to another: "Be humble and gentle. Be patient with each other, making allowance for each other's faults because of your love. Always keep yourselves united in the Holy Spirit, and bind yourselves together with peace" (Eph. 4:2–3 NLT).

Joseph is a beautiful example of extending grace to those who wronged him. When his brothers repented, he had a prime opportunity to retaliate. Instead, Joseph revealed himself to them and offered them grace and forgiveness. Even though his brothers' hatred had driven them to sell him as a slave, banishing him from home and family, Joseph returned their malice with love. He did so because of his firm belief in the sovereignty of God and his firsthand experience of God's gracious presence. Several times in the account of Joseph's life we find these words: "The LORD was with Joseph" (Gen. 39:2, 21, 23 NLT).

Because we have received God's boundless grace, we can grant grace to others. His grace is sufficient whatever our circumstances, and therefore we can trust God to work all things together—people may have meant it for evil, but God meant it for good. Because we see His hand in our lives, we have the strength to be patient, to make allowances for others, and to forgive.

━━━━━

"Where is God giving you opportunities to extend grace to others?"

━━━━━

If by faith you know Christ as your personal Savior, you are a recipient of God's grace. Just like the woman taken in adultery, you are no longer under condemnation. This grace, boundless as it is, does not give you license to continue practicing sin. The Lord told the woman to go and sin no more. Oswald Chambers advised, "Measure your growth in grace by your sensitiveness to sin."[4]

It is because you love God and understand His marvelous grace that you want to journey toward His heart and please Him in all that you do. As you travel, you have the privilege of experiencing His grace every day—which is always commensurate with your need. It is continually available as you ask for it at the throne of grace and as you abide in His Word. Because you have become a grace receiver, you can now be a grace giver. You are privileged to be on a gracious journey toward the heart of an amazingly gracious God.

May Thy rich grace impart
Strength to my fainting heart,
My zeal inspire;
As Thou has died for me,
O may my love to thee
Pure, warm, and changeless be,
A living fire![5]

FIFTEEN

His Manifold Goodness

The streams of God's goodness are so numerous,
and run so full, so strong, to all the creatures,
that we must conclude the fountain that is in
himself to be inexhaustible. We cannot conceive
how much good our God does every day, much
less can we conceive how good he is.

Matthew Henry[1]

I recall traveling to a country in which we were told that wherever we went, we had to be very careful about staying with our group. We were cautioned to keep our valuables with us at all times and to be alert when anyone approached us. Although the sights were very interesting, our visit was somewhat stressful because of our need to remain continually vigilant. The country was not noted for its goodness.

Another country we visited was extremely friendly and respectful. We were told that we did not need to worry about our safety or possessions. It was a *good* country. We did not have to preoccupy ourselves with thoughts of any impending danger. We could relax and enjoy our stay.

When we know that we are in an environment characterized by goodness, we are free from anxiety that someone is trying to do us harm. When we know that our journey is toward the heart of a good God, we may trust that He is leading us along good paths, to places where we will be privileged to see more clearly His immeasurable love for us.

Is God Good Enough?

Oh, that fruit is so tantalizing. And it will make me wise! I know God said not to eat it, but the serpent said I wouldn't die. I mean, he has to be right. If God really is good, He wouldn't withhold anything from us that would make us wise. I know that God is good—look at everything He has given us! It just doesn't make sense that He would keep us from something that would be such a benefit in our lives.

Such might have been Eve's thinking as she listened to Satan. I have heard this serpent's voice many times, with this same "logic." Very subtly I hear whispered in my thoughts, *Yes, God is good, but sometimes He's just not good enough. Otherwise, this would not be happening to you. Look, what you want is good. Why don't you go ahead and make it happen?*

Oswald Chambers described this insidious reasoning as a temptation to confuse what seems right with what is good:

> As soon as you begin to live the life of faith in God, fascinating and luxurious prospects will open up before you, and these things are yours by right; but if you are living the life of faith you will exercise your right to waive your rights, and let God choose for you. . . . Whenever *right* is made the guidance in the life, it will blunt the spiritual insight. The great enemy of the life of faith in God is not sin, but the good which is not good enough. The good is always the enemy of the best.[2]

It seemed good to Eve to eat the fruit, but it was not the best.

It seemed good to Sarai to encourage Abram to have a child by Hagar, but it was not the best.

It seemed good to Rebekah to assist Jacob in deceiving Isaac, but it was not the best.

The individuals in each instance affirmed the recognition that God is good—but it seemed He just wasn't performing up to speed, the way they'd been expecting. It seemed He wasn't quite good *enough*.

The disciples felt that way when their boat was being whipped around by a raging storm—and Jesus was sleeping! They woke Him up. With a hint of reproach they said, "Teacher, do You not care that we are perishing?" (Mark 4:38 NASB). My personal paraphrase reads, *Jesus, we're dying in this storm, and You're sound asleep! Sure, we know You're good. Yes, we know You love us. But You're not coming through for us right now! Come on, don't You care?*

After Martha and Mary called for Jesus, He "strolled" into Bethany. Martha met Him on the road and complained, "If You had been here, my brother would not have died" (John 11:21 NASB). My paraphrase reads, *Lord, I am in agony over the fact that You showed up late—too late! I don't know what I feel really—it just seems that if You really are good, and if You truly do love us, You would have come immediately.*

The elder brother felt some resentment when his father welcomed his prodigal brother home with a lavish party. *Honestly, father, I've been here all this time, doing my duty. I've always been good. I haven't rebelled and squandered my inheritance. I've never had a party. It's not fair! I know that you are good, but you have never been this good to me!*

The dear young woman sitting across from me was weeping. "I have a son and a daughter. I cannot have any more children, and my husband is opposed to adoption. The one thing I have always wanted in life was a house full of children—and I can't have them."

It's good to be wise, isn't it? It's good to want to be safe from a violent storm, isn't it? It's good for someone to be healed instead of dying early, isn't it? It's good to be good, isn't it? It's good to want a lot of children to love, isn't it? Then why doesn't God exercise His goodness on our behalf? God is good, but is He good enough?

═══

"When have you felt that God was not good enough?"

═══

What's Good About This?

Second Chronicles 16:9 depicts God in continuous activity on our behalf: "The eyes of the LORD search the whole earth in order to strengthen those whose hearts are fully committed to him" (NLT). God is always at work to do good in our lives. But it is sometimes hard to understand this truth because of the way we tend to define *good*. *My* definition of *good* is "anything that makes me happy and my life hassle-free." *God's* definition of *good* is "anything that makes me more like Jesus Christ and brings Him glory."

God's goodness is bound to all that is of eternal worth, to all that will bring us closer to conformity with His Son. Thus the Scriptures emphasize growth in the inner life: Paul's prayer in Ephesians 3:16 is for "mighty *inner strength* through his Holy Spirit"; in 2 Corinthians 4:16, he declares that "our *spirits* are being renewed every day" (NLT, italics added). Asaph declares in Psalm 73:26, "God remains the strength of my *heart*" (NLT, italics added). God is working for "love, joy, peace, patience, kindness, goodness, faithfulness, gentleness, and self-control" (Gal. 5:22–23 NLT).

The underlying purpose of God's good work is stated very clearly in Romans: "God knew what he was doing from the very beginning. He decided from the outset to shape the lives of those who love him along the same lines as the life of his Son" (Rom. 8:29 *The Message*). Our heavenly Father would like us to have a strong family resemblance!

God is more interested in developing our character than He is in manipulating our circumstances to make us happy. How did the Lord respond to the storm? He quieted the storm but rebuked the disciples for their lack of faith. It was a faith-building exercise. What was His primary concern in the death of Lazarus? God had much more in mind than healing—an incredible miracle that brought Him glory and brought many to belief in Him. What was Jesus' point regarding the unfair celebration for the prodigal son? The elder brother's relationship with his father was one of duty, not of love, and he needed to comprehend the deep love of his father for both sons. How does God respond to lost dreams for a family?

The young woman felt she knew what was best for her life, and she needed to learn to rest in whatever God chose to bring about in her future.

When we truly believe in the goodness of God, our perception of circumstances will change. Instead of questioning God's care for us, we will learn to trust that God loves us and is constantly at work for our good. Here is our guarantee: "We know that God causes everything to work together for the good of those who love God and are called according to his purpose for them" (Rom. 8:28 NLT). Had Eve believed this, she would have known that even when we are denied something we think is good, we may trust that God knows what is best for us.

> *God is more interested in developing our character than He is in manipulating our circumstances to make us happy.*

This was Ruth's belief—though she had lost her husband, she had found God. She loved Him and wanted to accomplish His purposes. As she sought shelter under His wings, she reflected the psalmist's declaration, "You are good, and do only good; teach me your principles" (Ps. 119:68 NLT).

A young woman I know married for the first time in her mid-thirties. At the wedding reception, many of her friends commented on the goodness of God in her life. Although she received their words graciously, in her heart she knew that even if she had never married, God was still good.

"Do you trust in God's goodness?"

What Does His Good Work Look Like?

Jesus said that He is the True Vine, His Father is the Gardener, and we are the branches. One of the major ways that God produces the eternal and the fruit of the Spirit in our lives is by pruning: "And he prunes the branches that do bear fruit so they will produce even more" (John 15:2 NLT). If I were a rosebush, I don't think I would like the sight of my owner coming at me with a sharp knife to lop off my stems! But the only way a rosebush will bloom is by pruning. So it is with us. We must be nipped, snipped, and thinned out so that we can blossom and produce the fruit of the Spirit.

My idea of learning patience, for example, is to go to a lovely place by a stream, open my Bible, and read in the Psalms for about twenty minutes. Then I rise up, and lo—I am patient and gentle. God's idea is to put me in an old house with three small children and a husband whose job keeps him out of the house. God's way tends to produce lasting results; my way lasts until I don't get my way. But God always presses for the best. In His goodness, He prunes us that we might begin to reflect His goodness.

That was Job's discovery. Job was "blameless, a man of complete integrity. He feared God and stayed away from evil" (Job 1:1 NLT). Why would God put a man like that through a season of severe pruning? George D. Watson observes of Job, "In his great sufferings, he died to his own religious life; died to his domestic affections; died to his theology; all his views of God's providence; he died to a great many things which in themselves were not sin, but which hindered his largest union with God."[3]

Job responded to the Lord,

> I know that you can do anything, and no one can stop you. You ask, "Who is this that questions my wisdom with such ignorance?" It is I. And I was talking about things I did not understand, things far too wonderful for me. . . . I had heard about you before, but now I have seen you with my own eyes. I take back everything I said, and I sit in dust and ashes to show my repentance. (Job 42:2–3, 5–6 NLT)

It was an extraordinary lesson for Job to learn. God wants us to see Him, to know Him, to be free from any trappings of religiosity. Pruning has nothing to do with correction, but everything to do with shaping and molding the eternal in us. God's goodness will prune us, and God's goodness will bless us.

"How willing are you to be pruned?"

Now I Have Seen Your Goodness

I feel that I often fail to acknowledge God's goodness in my life. I tend to focus on my struggles rather than on how good He is. Many years ago I began to pray that I would be aware of His manifold goodness to me.

A week before our thirty-fifth wedding anniversary, I was speaking at a conference. The musician, a trumpeter, played a beautiful arrangement of the hymn "God of Our Fathers." Tears filled my eyes, for that hymn was playing when I walked down the aisle as a young bride.

Afterward, I asked the musician why she had chosen that particular hymn. She replied, "About two weeks ago, I felt a prompting to learn to play 'God of Our Fathers' for performance at this seminar. I told the Lord that I already had my music planned, and I didn't have time to learn a new piece. But the prompting would not go away. So, out of obedience, I played it." At that moment I felt God's goodness toward me—*Cynthia, I love you, and I planned this special gift for your anniversary just to encourage you.*

On another occasion, Jack and I attended a conference and enjoyed the speaker immensely. I very much wanted to meet him and his wife, but there were always people around him. I still tend to be intimidated by speakers, so I contented myself simply with listening to his messages. One morning while we were driving to breakfast at that same conference, we spotted a couple walking alongside the road. Before we knew who they were, Jack stopped and asked if they would like a ride. Into our backseat came the speaker and his wife. It was quite natural for us to walk in together and share breakfast, and we had a lovely visit. On my way to the meeting afterward, the Lord whispered in my heart, *Cynthia, I arranged this meeting. This was from Me.*

═══
═══

*"Can you describe a recent experience of
God's goodness to you?"*

═══
═══

Nothing happens by coincidence or luck in our lives. God is working all things, trials as well as blessings, for our good.

God worked for Joseph's ultimate good through all of his circumstances. Paul testified to God's goodness from his prison cell: "And I want you to know, dear friends, that everything that has happened to me here has helped to spread the Good News. . . . And because of my imprisonment, many of the Christians here have gained confidence and become more bold in telling others about Christ" (Phil. 1:12, 14 NLT). The pioneer missionary in China, Hudson Taylor, would never have gone to the city of Ningpo if he had not been robbed and left destitute in Shanghai. He lived temporarily with the missionary community in Ningpo, and it was there that he found his wife, Maria. God is always working all things together for our good.

You do not have to experience a special hymn or meet someone prominent to know that God is good. His goodness is forever and endlessly communicated in the Cross. In sacrificing His Son for your redemption, He has proven His manifold goodness and immeasurable love. Can you ever be disappointed in Someone who has died for you? You are traveling a road on which you need not fear for your safety. He is your refuge, your fortress, and your protector. You are deeply loved, and your Father wants only what is good for you. He is committed to working all things together for your good. I pray that your journey will always be one of awe, holy love, and gratitude for His goodness.

> *Great things He hath taught us, great things He hath done,*
> *And great our rejoicing through Jesus the Son;*
> *But purer, and higher, and greater will be*
> *Our wonder, our transport, when Jesus we see.*[4]

SIXTEEN

His Absolute Sovereignty

> God transcends all limitations which time or space impose. He cannot be imprisoned either in time or space. In like manner, He knows all things perfectly. He is able to bring things to pass, even to create as He wills apart from means or material, and always in measureless perfection. . . . God has been styled "The Absolute," which is an attempt to express the fact that He exists eternally by no cause whatsoever outside Himself and that He alone is the sufficient cause of all that is.
>
> Lewis Sperry Chafer[1]

A friend of mine is a missionary in Mexico. For vacation one year, she and her husband took the family camping out in the Mexican countryside. They would enjoy the outdoors and save money on hotel expenses as well. The last night of their vacation, her husband promised, they would drive back into the city and treat themselves to a room in a nice hotel.

As the week passed, my friend increasingly looked forward to their hotel stay. She could hardly wait to take a hot shower, wash her hair, and sleep in a real bed with clean sheets in a temperature-controlled room.

When the day came, however, they were late breaking camp, and then it seemed that one thing after the next conspired against their reaching a hotel in time to get a room. After a few frustrating inquiries with no success, the husband decided it would be better if they went back to the campground and stayed there after all. They made the long drive back, set up camp all over again, and spent their final night in the rugged outdoors. She felt disappointed and frustrated, and she couldn't help feeling a little sorry for herself that things hadn't turned out the way they'd planned.

> *What looks like a disappointment or a setback may well be an important event in God's loving plan for our lives.*

The next day, they drove into the city and discovered that it had just been devastated by a severe earthquake. The hotel in which they had planned to stay was a shambles, and many of the guests had perished or been critically injured.

This is not to say that God always protects us from earthquakes. But there is always more to the picture than we can see, and only God sees all of it. What looks like a disappointment or a setback may well be an important event in God's loving plan for our lives. As we travel, it is important to remember that we hold the hand of a Father who has perfect knowledge of what lies ahead, and perfect intentions for what He will allow us to go through.

The Sovereign Creator

Years ago I heard a man from a foreign country pray out loud in his own language. I remember thinking on impulse, *How can God understand him?* A moment later, I felt foolish when I realized, of course, he was addressing the God of the universe, the God of all creation—language included! And not only does He understand every language, He even knows what we are going to say before we pray. This is our sovereign God—all-knowing and all-powerful.

Psalm 33 paints a majestic picture of our Creator:

> The LORD merely spoke,
> and the heavens were created.

He breathed the word,
　　and all the stars were born.
He gave the sea its boundaries
　　and locked the oceans in vast reservoirs.
Let everyone in the world fear the LORD,
　　and let everyone stand in awe of him.
For when he spoke, the world began!
　　It appeared at his command. (vv. 6–9 NLT)

The creation broadcasts God's sovereignty. I learned recently that the latest estimate of the number of stars in the galaxies of the visible universe is one sextillion. That is a one followed by twenty-one zeros! As I read this information, I thought of the verse, "He counts the stars and calls them all by name" (Ps. 147:4 NLT). Can there possibly be one sextillion names? Is He really aware of when every sparrow falls? Does He actually know the number of hairs on each person's head? Yes, because our God is infinite and knows all things.

It would be enough to stand in awe of God's power revealed in nature, but His creation of *us* is astounding as well. My oldest daughter, an audiologist, explained to me that the tiniest bones in the body are the hammer, the anvil, and the stirrup of the middle ear. The amazing thing is that these bones are the only ones in the entire human body that are fully formed at birth. Only God can create a being with a trio of tiny bones that will not grow inside a body full of other bones that will fully develop to maturity. The psalmist expressed this wonder:

You made all the delicate, inner parts of my body
　　and knit me together in my mother's womb.
Thank you for making me so wonderfully complex!
　　Your workmanship is marvelous—and how well I know it.
(Ps. 139:13–14 NLT)

"When do you usually feel amazement over God's creation?"

The Sovereign Overseer

A king rejects his wife because she disobeys him. He gives his servants permission to hold a beauty contest to select the young woman who will eventually become his new queen. A young Jewish girl is chosen for her beauty, and she impresses everyone who meets her—especially the king's eunuch in charge of the harem from whom she receives preferential treatment. She hides her Jewish heritage.

The wicked prime minister is furious because a certain Jewish man—the young woman's uncle, who raised her as his own daughter—will not violate his Hebrew faith and bow to him. He decides that the best way to deal with such dishonor is to manipulate the king into signing a decree to destroy this man along with his entire race.

The Jewish man sends a message to his adopted daughter, now the new queen, begging her to intercede with the king and challenging her with the thought, "And who knows whether you have not attained royalty for such a time as this?"

She accepts the challenge, but it has been a month since she has been asked to enter the king's presence—and the rule is, only the king initiates a visit. She asks her maidens, along with all the Jews in the capital city, to fast with her in preparation for her approach to the king. Drastic measures such as fasting are necessary because no one enters the king's presence uninvited. If anyone ventures to do so and the king does not immediately extend his golden scepter, that person will be killed instantly. So after the young queen fasts for three days, she walks up to the king's inner court, takes a deep breath as she opens the door to approach the king, and says to herself, "If I perish, I perish."

It just so happens that the king is delighted to see her. She invites him and the prime minister to a banquet. The king is having a wonderful time and asks his queen if she has a request. She replies by inviting him to another banquet the following day.

The prime minister is elated to be invited to the queen's luncheon. He's in popular standing with the king and the queen, and life seems to be going exceptionally well for him—except that impudent Jewish man is still refusing to honor him. He consults with his family, who suggest that he simply build a gallows, ask the king to hang the insufferable man the next day, and then go have a good time at the queen's second banquet. With this hanging to look forward to, the prime minister sleeps contentedly.

How easily we forget that He is the divine Overseer, in charge of the universe He Himself summoned forth.

But the king is not able to sleep that night. Since Nytol has not yet been invented, the king wakes up the court historian and asks him to read the boring, sleep-inducing book of records. Before drifting off, the king hears the record of how the Jewish man saved the king's life by foiling an attempted assassination plot.

The next morning the king wakes up planning to honor this man, and the prime minister wakes up planning to execute him. In the ultimate irony, the king orders the prime minister to honor the Jewish man by leading him on horseback through the city square. At the banquet, the queen exposes the prime minister's evil scheme and asks the king to revoke the decree.

The prime minister is hanged, the Jews are spared, and God's sovereignty reigns.

You have just read my *Reader's Digest* version of the book of Esther! It is a fascinating story and a beautiful example of how God orders and engineers circumstances to accomplish His purposes.

Esther was not chosen to be queen by chance. It was not a stroke of luck that the king embraced her after a month's absence instead of having her killed for her boldness. It was not by accident that Esther waited twenty-four hours before telling the king about Haman's evil schemes and the implications of the decree to annihilate the Jews. The king was awake in the night because God needed him to hear about Mordecai's faithfulness. It is just like the sovereign Lord to reverse Haman's plan so that Haman had to dress Mordecai in a royal robe, mount him on one of the king's horses, and lead him around the city square, shouting, "This is what happens to those the king wishes to honor!" It was the divine plan that the Jews were saved and Haman was killed.

So often it seems that events occur by accident or coincidence. When we are in the midst of challenging circumstances and fail to see evidence of God at work, we tend to question whether He is truly paying attention to what is happening. How easily we forget that He is the divine Overseer, in charge of the universe He Himself summoned forth.

From the viewpoint of a frightened Hebrew mother, she was sending her baby off in a basket down the Nile, because it was better than the certain death ordered by the Egyptian king.

But it was the divine plan that Pharaoh's daughter drew the baby Moses out of the water.

From the viewpoint of Ruth and Naomi, they were two unprotected women fated to spend the rest of their lives scrambling just to survive.

But it was the divine plan that Ruth "happened" into the field of Boaz.

From the viewpoint of Joseph, all his dreams were shattered when he was sold into slavery.

But it was the divine plan for him to be in Egypt.

From the viewpoint of the disciples, all their hopes were dashed when Jesus was crucified.

But it was the divine plan that Jesus purchase our redemption.

❦

"All the people of the earth are nothing compared to him," declared a humbled King Nebuchadnezzar after his seven-year chastening.

> He has the power to do as he pleases
>> among the angels of heaven
>> and with those who live on earth.
> No one can stop him or challenge him,
>> saying, "What do you mean by doing these things?"
>> (Dan. 4:35 NLT)

"Do you trust in God's sovereign control of your world?"

The Sovereign
with Good Purposes

Although it is important to understand that God is in charge and can do whatever He pleases, it is equally important to affirm that He is always acting for good purposes. He does not exercise His sovereignty in capricious displays of power. Job testified, "I know that Thou canst do all things, / And that no purpose of Thine can be thwarted" (Job 42:2 NASB).

I am secure because I know that a loving God is controlling this world.

As Job discovered, God's purposes are not always apparent, especially in the midst of the circumstances in which He chooses to accomplish them. I have wondered, for example, why God didn't take the Israelites straight into Canaan once He delivered them from Egypt. If He can do all things and no purpose of His can be hindered, then why did He allow them to wander in the wilderness for forty years?

But the wilderness exile was no deviation from His overall plan. God's ultimate purpose of bringing Israel into Canaan was accomplished—forty years later—but His will was not thwarted. And through the experience, the Israelites learned many priceless lessons about their disobedience and God's faithfulness.

In His sovereignty, God sometimes allows us to choose whether we will participate in His purposes, as with the Israelites going into Canaan. Other times, as with Joseph's kidnapping and slavery, God's sovereignty means that our circumstances are decided for us. This raises the question of how God's providence and our responsibility operate at the same time— which is certainly hard to comprehend. If God controls all, then do we have a choice? And if we have a choice, is God sovereign? Thankfully, we may turn to some godly thinkers for help with this dilemma:

> Upon such a subject, no man should be ashamed to acknowledge his ignorance. We are not required to reconcile the divine decrees and human liberty. It is enough to know that God has decreed all things which come to pass, and that men are answerable for their

actions. Of both these truths we are assured by the Scriptures; and the latter is confirmed by the testimony of conscience. . . . But the tie which connects the divine decrees and human liberty is invisible. "Such knowledge is too wonderful for us; it is high, we cannot attain unto it." If every thing in religion were level to the comprehension of reason, there would be no room for faith. It is better to believe humbly, than to reason presumptuously. And presumptuous all those reasonings may be called, which lead to the denial of the immutability of the divine counsels, or of the freedom of the human will; which make man a machine, and God the author of sin.[2]

Although I do not understand the mystery of what God ordains and what He permits, I believe wholeheartedly in the absolute sovereignty of God. I am secure because I know that a loving God is controlling this world. He is the only One who can redeem and bring *good* from all the suffering and evil. I also know that one day I must give an account of my life to God. I will answer for the choices I made. I can never say, "The devil made me do it," for God has delivered me from the rule of Satan so that I am no longer a slave of sin. And I cannot say, "God, why didn't *You* make me do it?" for He loves me too much to force me to obey Him.

Lewis Sperry Chafer commented on the freedom that God allows us:

> In respect to His permissive will, it is claimed, God determines not to hinder the course of action which His creatures pursue; but He does determine to regulate and control the bounds and the results of such actions. John Howe has said on this point: "God's permissive will is his will to permit whatsoever he thinks fit to permit, or, not to hinder; while what he so wills or determines so to permit, he intends also to regulate, and not to behold as an idle unconcerned spectator."[3]

In Jonah, we have an ideal example of how our sovereign Lord permits us to make choices while using the choices and their consequences to accomplish His purposes. Although God allowed Jonah to run away from his God-given mission, He certainly "regulated" Jonah's disobedience.

(I would call an extremely large fish a pretty effective regulator!) Even in Jonah's exercise of his free will, God's ultimate purpose was accomplished.

God is not an idle, unconcerned spectator. Sometimes I think we wish He were! He knows everything we are doing and will intervene as He pleases. With the Israelites, God led them and provided for them in their disobedience. God permitted them their free will, but He sovereignly cared for them. Forty years is not a problem to God, but forty years can certainly interrupt our lives. Understanding the importance of letting God be sovereign and letting Him choose for us is critical to how and where we journey. Will we sojourn in a whale? A wilderness? Or a king's castle?

===

"Where in your life do you find it difficult
to let God choose for you?"

===

The Sovereign
Who Redeems

God arranged for Esther to be queen. He knew what was ahead, and He placed everyone in position so that His purposes would not be thwarted. Still, we might wonder, why does God allow the Hamans of the world even to try to disrupt His plans? Why does He permit sin and evil?

Chafer observed that God's purposes are not simply to eliminate sin; otherwise He would have prevented it from ever getting a foothold:

> The permission of evil *continues* with every succeeding hour of human history. That which in His own counsels He did not hinder in the beginning, He does not hinder in all its subsequent development. The manifestation of evil must run its determined course and arrive at its determined ends. . . . It may be concluded, then, that sin is in the universe by the permission of God who hates it perfectly and who, being sovereign, had power to keep it from manifestation, had He chosen to do so. That He did not hinder the manifestation of sin, demonstrates that He, being what He is,

must have a purpose in view other than the averting of sin. Here as nowhere else in the affairs of the universe, the end justifies the means.[4]

It is a great consolation to me to know that God is in control, that He is superintending all of life for His ultimate purposes—to redeem and love us so that we can worship and glorify Him. God can take our bent for sin and the evil around us and cause it, in some way, to work for His good. He is a sovereign with redemptive purposes.

I talked with a young woman who viewed the universe as one in which God was not in control and evil could do as it pleased. People, therefore, were vulnerable to whatever might come into their lives with no hope that God was overseeing or controlling what was happening. In her mind, there was no all-powerful God watching, limiting, comforting, or redeeming the circumstances of our lives.

Only a sovereign Lord can orchestrate all the instruments that are playing in our lives to produce music of hope and significance.

If God is helpless and unable to control or accomplish His purposes, then He is not God. If He can be prevented from establishing His kingdom, He is not the Almighty. Satan cannot hinder God's plan. Satan has not defeated God. Incredibly, God even uses the enemy to accomplish His purposes.

The Scriptures record instances in which God allowed Satan to approach, but never conquer, His people. In the book of Job, God queried Satan, "Have you considered My servant Job?" Then the Lord gave Satan permission to test Job, within certain limits. What was the result? God used this trial to bring Job into a more intimate relationship with Himself.

In another instance, Jesus told Peter that Satan had asked permission to sift him like wheat. Again, God permitted Satan to touch one of His own for the ultimate accomplishment of His purpose. Peter was sifted, and although his faith faltered, what came forth was pure wheat; the chaff had been blown away. Peter was humbled, and he was strengthened. He was prepared to be used mightily by God.

The Lord used Satan in Paul's life, just as He did in Peter's. A messenger of Satan was sent to Paul to keep him from being conceited. The result? Paul was strengthened in endurance, trust, and a deeper experience of God's boundless grace.

How reassuring it is that God controls, and even uses, evil in this world for His purposes. Only a sovereign Lord can orchestrate all the instruments that are playing in our lives to produce music of hope and significance.

Oswald Chambers described the freedom of living in reliance upon God's sovereignty:

> If we accept the Lord Jesus Christ and the domination of His lordship, we also accept that nothing happens by chance, because we know that God orders and engineers circumstances; the fuss has gone, the amateur providence has gone, the amateur disposer has gone, and we know that "all things work together for good to those who love God."[5]

When we are tempted to question what God is up to in our lives, the psalmist reminds us not to presume to judge whether His purposes are good: "Who is able to advise the Spirit of the LORD? Who knows enough to be his teacher or counselor? Has the LORD ever needed anyone's advice? Does he need instruction about what is good or what is best?" (Isa. 40:13–14 NLT).

━━━━━

"Do you believe that God is using the hard things
in your life for His good purposes?"

━━━━━

When we doubt that we will be able to withstand what God allows in our lives, the apostle reminds us that we are not left helpless:

> But remember that the temptations that come into your life are no different from what others experience. And God is faithful. He will keep the temptation from becoming so strong that you can't stand up against it. When you are tempted, he will show you a way out so that you will not give in to it. (1 Cor. 10:13 NLT)

To know that God is exercising His loving authority in all He commands will bring peace into your life. You don't have to be in charge—God is! You may rest in God's rule and in His ability to lead you. You may be confident that nothing happens by chance and that the Lord is never surprised by your situation. Your only responsibility is to allow God to be sovereign in your life, to love Him, and to desire the accomplishment of His purposes in your life. You have the great privilege of watching God work all things together for good. You relinquish control to the only One worthy and able to exercise that control for the highest good.

I know that I cannot name one sextillion stars. I cannot create tiny little bones that enable a person to hear. Why should I attempt to control my life? There is only one God who can sovereignly reign with wisdom, compassion, and justice—and He is my Father, who is holding my hand on my journey.

This is my Father's world,
O let me ne'er forget
That though the wrong seems oft so strong,
God is the ruler yet.
This is my Father's world:
The battle is not done;
Jesus who died shall be satisfied,
And earth and heaven be one.[6]

SEVENTEEN

His
Perfect
Will

**Doing God's will is never hard. The only thing
that is hard is *not* doing His will.**

Oswald Chambers[1]

I've heard the story of a husband who wanted to surprise his wife with a very special birthday party. He sent out invitations to a small group of their close friends, asking them to be ready for a four-day trip to a destination that would be revealed only when they got there. He gave them specific instructions for what to pack—including black ties and tuxes and evening gowns—and when to be ready for the limousine pickup at their door. When the time came, the friends were whisked out to the airport. Together with the surprised birthday honoree, they boarded a private jet equipped with private sleeping areas for each couple.

They flew to New York where, that evening, they enjoyed dinner and a Broadway show. Afterward, they retired to their jet for a night's sleep and woke up in Rome the next morning. After taking in a few marvelous sights and enjoying a lavish midday meal, they were off to Paris, and then on to London, before returning home.

Imagine being treated to such a trip! You don't know exactly where it will take you, but you do know who is arranging it. You trust his judgment, so you are confident that no matter where the itinerary leads, you're in for a good time. You also know that he has your best interests in mind, and so you can feel safe that he will be looking out for your needs. The only information you are given at the beginning of the trip is what to pack, when the journey will begin, and the fact that you will travel with people whose company you enjoy. The suspense of discovering where you are headed is a thrill. When the trip begins and you get the first taste of what an incredible adventure it will be, you are hooked. This is the experience of a lifetime!

"I will guide you along the best pathway for your life," says the Lord. "I will advise you and watch over you" (Ps. 32:8 NLT). Our God does not give us a detailed map of what lies ahead and will happen in each of our lives. But He has perfect knowledge of everything we will experience. He has given us the assurance that every step will bring us closer to our ultimate destination, His heart. As we accept His invitation to journey with Him, to depend upon His Guidebook for clear direction, and to be sensitive to His daily prompting in the choices we face, we may rest in the knowledge that He will guide us according to His perfect will.

Knowing the Will of God

From the very beginning, God let His will be known: "The LORD God placed the man in the Garden of Eden to tend and care for it. But the LORD God gave him this warning: 'You may freely eat any fruit in the garden except fruit from the tree of the knowledge of good and evil. If you eat of its fruit, you will surely die'" (Gen. 2:15–17 NLT).

> *He has given us the assurance that every step will bring us closer to our ultimate destination, His heart.*

Although the Lord instructed Adam and Eve concerning how they were to live in the garden, they decided to eat the forbidden fruit. Although His way is always the right way, our gracious God will not make us obey His will. He gives us a choice.

God does not ask us to understand His ways in order to accept them; He simply asks us to say yes to Him. When we do, He provides everything we need to live according to His will. He promises to direct us, to advise us, to watch over us. God wants us to do His will more than we want to do it!

"How do I know God's will?" is a familiar question. Just as God spoke His word to Adam, we have His Word today. Much of His will is revealed in Scripture. Do you want to know God's will? Then read the following passages:

> "You must love the Lord your God with all your heart, all your soul, and all your mind." This is the first and greatest commandment. A second is equally important: "Love your neighbor as yourself." (Matt. 22:37–39 NLT)

> God knew what he was doing from the very beginning. He decided from the outset to shape the lives of those who love him along the same lines as the life of his Son. (Rom. 8:29 *The Message*)

> Don't copy the behavior and customs of this world, but let God transform you into a new person by changing the way you think. Then you will know what God wants you to do, and you will know how good and pleasing and perfect his will really is. (Rom. 12:2 NLT)

> God wants you to be holy, so you should keep clear of all sexual sin. (1 Thess. 4:3 NLT)

> Always be joyful. Keep on praying. No matter what happens, always be thankful, for this is God's will for you who belong to Christ Jesus. (1 Thess. 5:16–18 NLT)

> There is really only one thing worth being concerned about. Mary has discovered it—and I won't take it away from her. (Luke 10:42 NLT)

God's will is for us to love Him and, through Him, to love others. His purpose for us is to have a strong resemblance to Jesus Christ. He wants us to seek His kingdom, and to resist the pressure of the world's influence. He desires our holiness. God asks that we be joyful, prayerful, and thankful. He wants our primary concern to be consistently sitting at His feet, as Mary did. These are only a few of the many passages God has given us with specific guidance for the kind of life He wants us to lead. In many choices we face, we have clear instruction for what God wants.

In areas where the instructions are not spelled out or we are confused about what to do, we can ask these questions:

- If I make this choice, will it be an expression of my love for God?
- Will it show others that I love them?
- Will it promote my holiness?
- Will it hinder my walk with God?
- (Courtesy of Adam and Eve): If I eat this fruit (or take this path), will it please God?

A young woman's husband left her after many years of marriage. He said that he no longer loved her, and he wanted her to initiate divorce proceedings. Her friends and family were encouraging her to go ahead with the divorce. As we talked, she asked how she could know the will of God. The best counsel I could give her at that time was, "Ask God the question, 'What will please You, Lord?'"

God does not ask us to understand His ways in order to accept them; He simply asks us to say yes to Him.

A wise person observed, "To know the will of God, we should have no will of our own." We cannot determine the will of God by feelings or by the counsel of others until we have offered that counsel to the Lord for His confirmation. Our hearts must be in neutral concerning our path ahead, and we must be eager to listen to the voice of the Lord in Scripture or as He speaks in our hearts. Abiding and praying, which He has asked us to do, are keys to a continual understanding of His will for us.

The psalmist gave us a beautiful prayer for asking God to reveal His will:

> Show me the path where I should walk, O LORD;
> point out the right road for me to follow.

> Lead me by your truth and teach me,
>> for you are the God who saves me.
>> All day long I put my hope in you. (Ps. 25:4–5 NLT)

This needs to be our ardent prayer: "Lord, I want to do only Your will. Show me and lead me." If we truly want to know and to do the will of God, then He will always guide us to the best path.

"Do you practice abiding and praying as the context
in which you seek to know God's will?"

I have learned that He leads in many different ways. Some ways are very clear; others are much more subtle. Unfortunately, He does not reveal His will to us by writing it out in large letters in the sky—I wish He would! On many occasions I have asked the Lord for direction, but from my viewpoint, it seems I have not received a specific reply. But that doesn't mean I am left without hope of knowing the will of God. Here are some wise principles I have learned from Oswald Chambers that have proven very helpful in my life.

In many choices we face, we have clear instruction for what God wants.

When in Doubt, Don't

> Never run before God's guidance. If there is the slightest doubt, then He is not guiding. Whenever there is doubt—*don't*.[2]

This principle has helped me greatly. Philippians 4:6–7 tells me that as I pray about everything, I will experience His peace. If I have a nagging little doubt and I don't have a "settledness" in my heart, then I know I should not make that choice. The nudge may indicate a permanent no or perhaps a not-at-this-time no, but either way it is a useful guideline for making decisions.

If You Begin to Debate, Quit

> Is my ear so keen to hear the tiniest whisper of the Spirit that I know what I should do? . . . He does not come with a voice like

thunder; His voice is so gentle that it is easy to ignore it. The one thing that keeps the conscience sensitive to Him is the continual habit of being open to God on the inside. When there is any debate, quit. "Why shouldn't I do this?" You are on the wrong track. There is no debate possible when conscience speaks. At your peril, you allow one thing to obscure your inner communion with God. Drop it, whatever it is, and see that you keep your inner vision clear.[3]

Here is a good reason to abide. Jesus tells us in John 8:31–32, "If you abide in My word, then you are truly disciples of Mine; and you shall know the truth, and the truth shall make you free" (NASB). In abiding, I begin to hear and know His voice. I read His words, and I know His thoughts. Then I am open and sensitive to His voice in my heart. When He prompts me, I need to obey. If I begin to question or refute His voice, then I know I am not open to His will and I am heading in the wrong direction.

Keep Going Unless He Checks

To be so much in contact with God that you never need to ask Him to show you His will, is to be nearing the final stage of your discipline in the life of faith. When you are rightly related to God's will, it is a life of freedom and liberty and delight, you *are* God's will, and all your common-sense decisions are His will for you unless He checks. You decide things in perfect delightful friendship with God, knowing that if your decisions are wrong He will always check; when He checks, stop at once.[4]

A young woman was frustrated with the Lord, for she had prayed and asked for guidance about which college she should attend. She never really heard from the Lord, but continued in her applications and finally chose a college *on her own*. Things were going well, but she was a little resentful that God had not specifically guided her. But is that true? In Psalm 32:8, God promises to watch over us. *If we truly want the will of God and are listening for His voice,* then He will not let us make a mistake. He will *check* us if we are moving in the wrong direction. Often I pray, "Lord, I want only Your will, so since I haven't specifically heard from You, I am going to keep going on this path, for it seems right. I will be sensitive to Your check or Your closing of a door."

"When has God checked you in a choice you were about to make?"

Trust God's Leading

Never revise your decisions, but see that you make your decisions in the light of the high hour.[5]

Once we have felt the Lord prompt our hearts, we must trust that we heard His truth. James 1:5 exhorts us, "If you need wisdom—if you want to know what God wants you to do—ask him, and he will gladly tell you. He will not resent your asking" (NLT). After receiving guidance, we don't need to doubt or wrestle with whether we made the right choice.

Recently, I was faced with a very hard decision. After much prayer and desire to do only what the Lord wanted, I heard His voice, and I chose a certain course. Later, I began to question whether I had done the right thing. I doubted *after* the decision, not before. But I needed to remember that my heart was open to do only His will, and that God could have checked me at any time. I could rest that I had chosen His way, and that I did not need to revise my decision.

Doing the Will of God

Jeremiah, the prophet: O King, I beg you to listen to what the Lord God almighty, the God of Israel, says. Surrender to the Babylonians. Go out to them, and you and your family will live. If you obey the Lord, the city will not be burned, and it will go well with you.

King Zedekiah: I fear that the Babylonians will turn me over to the Judeans who have defected, and they will abuse me.

Jeremiah: You will not be handed over to them if you choose to do as God has directed. You and your family will be spared.

Instead of trusting God, Zedekiah fled from the city. He was captured by the Chaldeans and brought before King Nebuchadnezzar. The Scriptures record what happened:

> There the king of Babylon pronounced judgment upon Zedekiah. He made Zedekiah watch as they killed his sons and all the nobles of Judah. Then he gouged out Zedekiah's eyes, bound him in chains, and sent him away to exile in Babylon. Meanwhile, the Babylonians burned Jerusalem, including the palace, and tore down the walls of the city. (Jer. 39:5–8 NLT)

God had made it very clear to Zedekiah what he should do. God wanted to guide him through a difficult situation, and He sent Jeremiah to make His will clear. Zedekiah could never say to God, "If only You had told me what to do!" There is certainly a high cost to disobedience. Zedekiah's last visual memory was seeing his sons killed. Could all of his pain have been avoided? Yes, God had told him what to do.

━━━

"What helps you to discern God's will?"

━━━

How we grieve God when we choose our own way, and how we suffer needlessly. Since God is sovereign and all His purposes will be fulfilled, His purposes are not dependent on our personal cooperation.

God's plan for the Israelites after liberation from Egypt was to bring them into Canaan, a land flowing with milk and honey. He offered it to the first generation, but it was not their choice. The second generation of Israelites went into Canaan, and the first generation missed out on God's will and blessing.

God's intention was for Jerusalem to be overthrown and for Zedekiah to be taken prisoner. God's plan was for him and his family to live in exile. But God also allowed Zedekiah to choose for himself, and the king missed out on the safety God offered through Jeremiah.

God will not make us obey Him. We demonstrate our love for Him when we keep His commands voluntarily. God gives us the *choice* to do His will.

It Is Harder Not to Do God's Will

Balak's message to Balaam: I am the king of Moab, and this vast horde of people have come into my land and are threatening me. You're a prophet—come and curse them for me.

God to Balaam: Do *not* go with these men. You are *not* to curse these people, for I have blessed them.

Balaam to the messengers: I cannot go with you. The Lord will not let me!

Balak's message to Balaam: Please reconsider. Here are my distinguished messengers with much money. I'll do anything you ask. Just come and curse these people!

Balaam to the messengers: I cannot do anything against the will of the Lord, but stay here and I will see if the Lord has *anything else* to say to me.

God to Balaam: Since the men are here, go with them. But do only what I tell you to do.

> I think that He gives us this liberty only after revealing His will to us first, in some definite manner. We are accountable for our choices.

I get uptight every time I read this passage. God could not have been any clearer about what He wanted Balaam to do. But Balaam pouted to the messengers and said in essence, "I want to go with you, but the Lord won't let me." Balak continued to appeal to Balaam's pride and greed. When he was approached again, Balaam started to give in by saying that he would go back to the Lord and check to see if He had any additional thoughts. What was Balaam doing? *What else* could the Lord say besides "Do not go"? I want to ask Balaam, "What is it about *no* that you don't understand?"

Balaam knew the will of the Lord; he just didn't like it. He wanted to try to bend the will of the Lord to his will. An incredible lesson appears here because God granted Balaam permission to go. God will often allow us to follow our own desires. I wish He wouldn't do that! But I think that He gives us this liberty only *after* revealing His will to us first, in some definite manner. We are accountable for our choices.

The rest of this story is great. Balaam went to Moab, encountered the displeasure of the angel of the Lord, heard his donkey speak, built altars for sacrifices, but was divinely restrained from cursing Israel. In fact, he could only bless them. Balaam is a good example of someone who would probably agree that it is harder *not* to do the will of God.

❧

We learn from Balaam that knowing the will of God is no guarantee of doing it. Our hearts must be set, as Jesus demonstrated and as the psalmist described in Psalm 40:8: "I take joy in doing your will, my God, for your law is written on my heart" (NLT).

When we are abiding and have His Word in our hearts, we take special joy in *doing* the will of God. Abiding keeps us motivated so that we always want to please God. There is great joy in doing what we know God wants us to do. Amy Carmichael quoted a fellow missionary, "Joy is simply perfect acquiescence in God's will, because the soul delights itself in God Himself."[6]

When we do *not* do what we know God wants, there is unrest. I know, for I have been there many times. When God asks me to forgive, to humble myself, to reach out to someone, to discipline myself to teach or write, and I don't do it, I am not content. It is harder *not* to do the will of God.

———

"Where do you find joy in doing God's will?"

———

God created you, purchased you, loves you and, more than any other being, knows what is the very best for you. He is a loving Father who wants to mold and fashion you into His child, who rests in His sovereignty and trusts in His ways. His will for you is to be intimate with Him, to be like the Lord Jesus, to bring Him glory. He delights in guiding you and watching over you. He wants you to understand that it is much harder, and too costly, *not* to do His will. He wants your hand in His as you journey so that you are always in the center of His perfect will.

The following prayer by Saint Thérèse of Lisieux has been on a bookmark in my Bible for the last two years. God used it in a very special way in my life when I was struggling with His will. His question to me was, *Cynthia, do you want the whole lot?* It is a prayer of abandonment. May it encourage you to say yes to whatever He asks of you:

> My God, I choose the whole lot. No point in becoming a saint by halves. I'm not afraid of suffering for your sake; the only thing I'm afraid of is clinging to my own will. Take it, I want the whole lot, everything whatsoever that is your will for me.[7]

> *Praise to the Lord, who o'er all things so wondrously reigneth,*
> *Shelters thee under His wings, yes, so gently sustaineth!*
> *Has thou not seen*
> *How all thy longings have been*
> *Granted in what He ordaineth?*[8]

EIGHTEEN

His Incomparable Ways

Be still, my soul! The Lord is on thy side;
Bear patiently the cross of grief or pain;
Leave to thy God to order and provide;
In every change He faithful will remain.
Be still, my soul! the best, thy heavenly Friend
Through thorny ways leads to a joyful end.[1]

Consider a tour guide who meticulously and with loving care plans a personalized trip for each individual who signs on. He has unique ways of conducting his tour and unconventional methods of travel. It may include hiking, flying, cruising, driving jeeps, bicycling, or cross-country skiing. When you register for his tour, you are told to be ready for anything! Those who choose this guide testify to his expertise and the adrenaline-boosting excitement that always accompanies traveling with him. Many people are hesitant to go on tour with him, however, for the unexpected and the paradoxical are the norm. He has a reputation for the uncommon, yet his personal attention is said to have no equal. He majors in providing profitable, unusual life experiences—his way.

God's Ways
Are Not Our Ways

Joshua: Here we are, Lord. We have all crossed the Jordan River, and we are finally in Canaan! We are ready to conquer Jericho. The archers are prepared, and the spears are freshly sharp-ened. We're ready to climb the walls and do battle.

> *"Are You sure this is the best way?"*

The Lord: Joshua, the approach I have in mind is a little different from what you're proposing. Here's what I want you to do. Take the army, the ark, and the priests, with trumpets, and march around Jericho once a day for six days. It will only take you about thirty minutes, and then you can have the rest of the day off. On the seventh day, march around seven times. Then have the priests blow the trumpets, which will be the signal for the people to let loose with a mighty shout. When that happens, the wall of the city will fall down flat.

Joshua: Lord, with all due respect, Sir, are You aware of how thick that wall is? I've fought a lot of battles, and I have *never* seen a wall go down by shouting! It makes no sense to me. We've got a lot at stake here. Are You *sure* this is the best way?

***

Gideon: Yes, Lord, You can count on me. Even though the Midianites are as numerous as locusts, I will lead the army against them.

The Lord: Gideon, you have too many men. Let those who are afraid depart.

Gideon: Well, Lord, twenty-two thousand men just left. I now have ten thousand ready to do battle.

The Lord: There are still too many. Bring them down to the spring, and I will sort out who will go with you by observing how they drink.

[Gideon waits and watches.]

The Lord: Now, take these three hundred men, and send the others home.

Gideon: Lord, three hundred men—against countless thousands? This doesn't make sense! Are You *sure* this is the best way?

❧❦❧

Goliath stands nine feet nine inches tall. His coat of armor weighs about 125 pounds. His helmet is solid bronze. The head of his spear alone weighs about 15 pounds. Walking immediately ahead of him, an armor bearer carries a huge shield.

The enormous figure steps to the edge of the valley. He taunts the armies of Israel assembled on the other side. He asks for a one-on-one fight to settle their conflict.

Astonishment ripples through the ranks. "One Israelite soldier in a contest with this murderous giant? Who can stand against such a man?" The Israelites are terrified.

A shepherd boy, lithe and tanned and simply dressed, steps forward.

(My thoughts if I had been there): *Wait! No, Lord, You can't allow a teenager to go into battle with a seasoned, gigantic warrior. Stop him! He is only a shepherd boy. He has no weapons, only a sling. It's not right! Didn't You just have him anointed—and now You're going to let him be killed? This is not a good idea. Are You* sure *this is the best way?*

❧❦❧

Mary waits with the donkey while Joseph inquires about a place for them to stay the night. Her time is very near.

(My thoughts if I had been in Mary's place): *Lord, it has not been an easy journey to Bethlehem. But we are here, and soon Your Son will be born. But I'm feeling a little confused. I certainly trust You, and I am Your servant, but I don't understand why there is no room. It seems that You at least could provide a room—I mean, this is Your Son. Are You* sure *this is the best way?*

❧❦❧

Jesus, by the Sea of Galilee, recruiting His disciples.

(My thoughts if I had been there): *Lord, You can't choose fishermen! I mean, if You have only three years to train these men, then You need some upbeat, presentable, scholarly types. Men who have an education and relate well to people. Well, okay, one fisherman might be all right, but You don't need four of them! And You're planning to make them Your close-in group. You know*

171

what I really think? You're making a mistake. Fishermen will not make good disciples. Are You sure this is the best way?

✿

Paul, kneeling in prayer, asking God to remove a burden from him.

(My thoughts to God on his behalf): *Lord, this dear man goes through so much! It seems that he is in prison more than he is out of prison. And he is always being beaten—with rods, whips, even a stoning! He is keenly acquainted with shipwrecks, and he has spent a day or so in the sea. The Jews are not his friends, the Gentiles are not all that friendly to him either, and even some of the Christians hurt him. And he's always encountering false teachers. He's been hungry, thirsty, cold, hot, and sleepless. He has a great heart for the church and suffers when they suffer. Now, Lord, I think that is enough for anyone to go through! But on top of all of this, You send him a thorn in the flesh! Doesn't the poor man have enough problems? It doesn't make sense to me. Do You think it is right to do this to him? Are you sure this is the best way?*

═══

"Is there a circumstance in your life that is causing you to ask the Lord, 'Are You sure this is the best way?'"

═══

✿

The Lord, responding to the question, "Are You *sure* this is the best way?":

"My thoughts are completely different from yours," says the LORD. "And my ways are far beyond anything you could imagine. For just as the heavens are higher than the earth, so are my ways higher than your ways and my thoughts higher than your thoughts." (Isa. 55:8–9 NLT)

Lord, how true. Your ways are not our ways! And I am thankful that they are not. Your ways are higher—they bring You glory, they teach us about You, they make us like Christ, and they always have an eternal impact. Our ways are self-absorbed—they call attention to ourselves, they are designed to eliminate any discomfort, and they are focused on the immediate. To us, our ways seem best, and Your ways seem perplexing and hard. I know that trials are not optional while we journey here. Those who know You experience pain, and those who do not walk with You experience physical and emotional distress also. While any of us are in the world, there will be tribulation. But, Lord, what are You after? What do You want to accomplish with Your ways?

"Which of your ways need to yield to God's ways?"

God's Ways Accomplish His Purposes

J. C. Ryle described some of the *why* behind God's ways: "Through affliction He teaches us many precious lessons that otherwise we would never learn. By affliction He shows us our emptiness and weakness, draws us to the throne of grace, purifies our affections, weans us from the world, and makes us long for heaven."[2]

Solomon is one of the very few people in Scripture who apparently did not endure many trials. But at the end of his life, he turned away from God. I wonder if there is a connection?

Trials are necessary to keep us dependent upon God and to keep us from thinking that we can live life in our own strength. It was only when I was pressed with three small children, a busy husband, and rodent houseguests that I recognized my emptiness and weakness and was ready to draw near the throne of grace. I realized that since life could not be lived on my terms (rat-free, husband home in the evenings, perfect children), I needed to do something in order to receive God's strength, comfort, and love in the midst of my turmoil. Without those trials, I never would have surrendered my life to God. I never would have begun to trust the Lord wholeheartedly. At that time, His ways drew me to Him. Ever since then, they have continued to keep me dependent upon Him.

The prayer of Moses in Exodus 33:13 indicates that experiencing God's ways leads us to a greater knowledge of Him: "Now therefore, I pray Thee, if I have found favor in Thy sight, let me know Thy ways, that I may know Thee" (NASB). We may be confident, therefore, that our surrender will surely bring us closer to the heart of our Father. Gary Thomas observes, "To really surrender, then, we need to learn to stop measuring our trials against our comforts, and instead measure our trials against their potential to draw us nearer to God."[3]

―――――

"Are you going through a trial that is—or could be—
drawing you closer to the heart of God?"

―――――

God's Ways Teach Us Trust

Any experience that teaches us to relinquish our own ways in favor of God's ways is an experience rich in opportunities for learning how to walk more closely with Him. Listen to Paul's account of a harrowing time in his life:

> I think you ought to know, dear friends, about the trouble we went through in the province of Asia. We were crushed and completely overwhelmed, and we thought we would never live through it. In fact, we expected to die. But as a result, we learned not to rely on ourselves, but on God who can raise the dead. (2 Cor. 1:8–9 NLT)

The Message paraphrases verse 9, "As it turned out, it was the best thing that could have happened. Instead of trusting in our own strength or wits to get out of it, we were forced to trust God totally—not a bad idea since he's the God who raises the dead!"

This is really what God is after: a firsthand, seeing-with-our-own-eyes encounter with Him.

Although God's ways can at times be overwhelming, they are always redemptive. To learn the trustworthiness of God and the freedom of not having to rely on our own strength is indeed a costly as well as a priceless lesson. It is so important to God that we learn to trust Him implicitly that He will risk His relationship with us in order for us to learn how to live this way.

We looked at God's pruning of Job as evidence of His goodness and commitment to our growth. In a sense, God drew the line and said, "Job, I want you to *see* Me, to know Me intimately. I want you to understand that *I am the Lord*. This is so important to Me that I am willing to put you on the ash heap and reduce you to silence so that your relationship with Me is the highest and best."

Listen to Job's remarkable response to God's ways with him:

> I admit I once lived by rumors of you;
>> now I have it all firsthand—from my own eyes and ears!
> I'm sorry—forgive me. I'll never do that again, I promise!
>> I'll never again live on crusts of hearsay, crumbs of rumor.
> (Job 42:5–6 *The Message*)

God's ways with Job seem beyond explanation—but they demonstrate that He is always after the very best in our journey with Him. Job's life was totally transformed. His walk with God was richer, deeper, freer. His relationship with God was authentic and natural. God's way, though extremely painful, enabled Job to experience God firsthand. This is really what God is after: a *firsthand, seeing-with-our-own-eyes encounter with Him*. This knowledge of God is possible only through His ways. But for anyone who experiences the living God in a firsthand encounter through affliction, the burden is tempered by the blessing.

———

"Can you describe a firsthand, seeing-with-your-own-eyes encounter with God in a painful experience?"

———

God's Ways
Develop Endurance

"Dear brothers and sisters, whenever trouble comes your way," James counseled, "let it be an opportunity for joy. For when your faith is tested, your endurance has a chance to grow. So let it grow, for when your endurance is fully developed, you will be strong in character and ready for anything" (James 1:2–4 NLT).

Personally speaking, I have always had trouble with these verses. How can I be joyful about the fact that I'm going through trials? I'm joyful when I can get out of bed in the morning without having to hit the snooze alarm! So how on earth can I live the way James told me?

Jerry Bridges helps answer this question when he comments, "It is not the adversity considered in itself that is to be the ground of our joy. Rather, it is the expectation of the results, the development of our character, that should cause us to rejoice in adversity."[4]

> *For anyone who experiences the living God in a firsthand encounter through affliction, the burden is tempered by the blessing.*

God's ways with each of us are personally fashioned to produce in us the character of the Lord Jesus. God uses our circumstances to mold us into the image of His Son. He has purchased us, redeemed us, and adopted us. As we have seen earlier, His good ways are designed to increase our family resemblance.

It was for the joy set before Jesus that He endured the Cross. He is our example of endurance so that we do not grow weary and lose heart. If Jesus had to endure, so must we. To *endure* means "to remain firm under suffering or misfortune without yielding—to bear, to continue."[5] As we take on His likeness, we will learn to rejoice in trials because they teach us to endure—and continual endurance results in strong character.

One of our adult children went through a hard time of testing, and after much struggle emerged stronger and more dependent on God. Several months later, when encountering another trial, this child told us, "You know, as difficult as that time was, I survived it and, in the process, learned a lot. Now, with this new trial I am not fearful of what is ahead because I know I can endure." This young person was ready for anything the journey might bring.

James assures us that our endurance does not go unnoticed: "God blesses the people who patiently endure testing. Afterward they will receive the crown of life that God has promised to those who love him" (James 1:12 NLT). I don't know exactly what the crown of life will be like, but it sounds pretty special. This crown is one example of God's incomparable ways. He strengthens us *in* the process of enduring, and He blesses us *for* enduring. God is honored and pleased when we endure trials. And we are released from the despairing thought, *I can't keep going*. This is a needed lesson for our pilgrimage.

———

"What good results can you see in your life of yielding to God's ways?"

———

God's Ways Are the Best Ways

As we comprehend God's loving purposes behind His choices for how we travel, we will increasingly affirm that His ways are higher than our ways because His ways are the best ways.

Why did God want the Israelites to walk around Jericho and "shout" the wall down? Once Israel arrived in Canaan, God needed to strengthen their faith, test their obedience, and encourage their leader, Joshua. Jericho was likely the most impregnable city in Canaan, and therefore it was crucial that God show Himself mighty on their behalf as they entered the land. They were His children, and He was in charge of the plans and the outcome. Since He was fighting for them, they could not lose. In fact, victory would come easily! Witnessing an impenetrable wall reduced to rubble by shouting would increase anyone's faith, and that was what God intended. It was the best way.

> *God imposed a restraint upon Paul to keep him from exalting himself. Pride could have become the very thing that would destroy Paul's ministry.*

Why did God send Gideon into battle with the Midianites supported by a paltry three hundred men? He wanted to increase the Israelites' faith by demonstrating to them that His strength was not dependent upon numbers. He did not want Israel to boast that *they* had won the battle. God wanted only a few good men so that He would receive glory and Israel would trust Him. It was the best way.

Why did God allow David, a young shepherd, to venture out into the valley alone to kill Goliath? Again, God needed to remind Israel that

He is the One who gives victory. It comes not by might or power, but by His Spirit. God could have used anyone to conquer the Philistines. But David was God's chosen to be king. In defeating Goliath, David won the favor of the people. But in that heroic act, David attracted the attention of Saul, who eventually turned against him when he perceived David's rising popularity as a threat to his throne. Thus began years of persecution from Saul—years of testing and trials that God used to teach David valuable lessons in preparation for his royal leadership. How else could David learn dependence upon the Lord for deliverance? How else could he experience God's protection? How else could he learn of God's love? How else could he mature? God's way was the best way.

Why wouldn't God provide a room for Mary to give birth to His own Son? The fact that Jesus had a manger instead of a crib tells us much about the character of our Lord. He is humble, unlike a human king who must have crowns and elegant robes and jewels. Earthly riches were not necessary to validate His rule. He became like us so that He could be our faithful High Priest who sympathizes with our weaknesses. We are drawn to Him because we know He understands us firsthand. He was not pretentious. He lived simply. God's way was best.

> *God knows what He is doing. He has His ways for you, and they are higher and better than what you would settle for on your own.*

Why did Jesus choose fishermen for disciples? Why did He choose Peter, who failed Him, and Judas, who betrayed Him? Why did He choose a band of men who argued about which one would be first in His kingdom? Why did He choose followers who had bad reputations? If Jesus could love and disciple those individuals, He can love and disciple you and me! His message is clear and encouraging. His way was best.

Why did Paul, with all his afflictions, suffer a thorn in the flesh? Of course, even with all that Paul went through, he was not the only one who was beaten or stoned or shipwrecked. James was killed; Peter and John were flogged; Stephen was stoned to death; Silas was beaten with Paul. Persecution was the norm for any outspoken Christian in that day. But Paul was unique among the apostles in the gift of special revelations that had been granted to him. He had literally been taken up into paradise and told inexpressible and astounding things. Because of that incredible experience, God imposed a restraint upon Paul to keep him from exalting himself. Pride could have become the very thing that would destroy Paul's ministry. God's way was best.

Francis de Sales encouraged us that we may safely trust God in His loving purposes for every circumstance we go through:

> Do not look forward to the changes and chances of this life in fear. Rather look at them with full hope that as they arise, God, whose you are, will deliver you out of them. He has kept you hitherto; do you but hold fast to His dear hand, and He will lead you safely through all things; and when you cannot stand, He will bear you in His arms. . . . Do not look forward to what may happen tomorrow. The same everlasting Father who cares for you today will take care of you tomorrow, and every day. Either He will shield you from suffering, or He will give you unfailing strength to bear it. Be at peace, then, put aside all anxious thoughts and imaginations.[6]

God knows what He is doing. He has His ways for you, and they are higher and better than what you would settle for on your own. They bring Him glory and accomplish His purposes in your life. He longs to show Himself mighty on your behalf. He wants you to know that His ways are always best, even though they may appear to be bewildering or unfair. Because He loves you, you may rejoice in walking by faith instead of by sight. Because He is your Guide, you may look forward to an exciting journey. "How do You want me to handle this wall, Lord—shout, sing, or climb? If it is just You and me, I am confident of victory—giants are not a problem. You sleep in mangers and socialize with fishermen; I trust You. I know that even the thorns are for my good, for only in my weakness can Your strength be perfected." His incomparable ways make for an incomparable journey.

Day by day and with each passing moment,
Strength I find to meet my trials here;
Trusting in my Father's wise bestowment,
I've no cause for worry or for fear.
He whose heart is kind beyond all measure
Gives unto each day what He deems best—
Lovingly, its part of pain and pleasure,
Mingling toil with peace and rest.[7]

NINETEEN

His
Abundant
Comfort

Trials make more room for comfort. Great hearts are made from great troubles. The shovel of trouble digs the reservoir of comfort deeper and makes room for more comfort.

Charles H. Spurgeon[1]

I'll never forget the time that Jack and I were flying home from a ministry trip to Australia. We were on an older plane from a fleet belonging to an overseas airline. On the overhead screen, a chart kept us posted on how far along we had advanced in our flight path. By the middle of the night, we had reached our midpoint over the Pacific Ocean. That's when we hit the storm.

The next twenty-five minutes seemed to drag on for hours. Like a child seizing a rattle, the storm shook our plane, tossing us up and down, back and forth, in a crazy and violent series of sudden drops and sideways lurches. There were awful creaking and wrenching sounds, and I asked Jack what they were. It was the plane's metal, straining and shifting under the terrific pressure. I thought the plane would surely fall apart.

I've been through some harrowing flights (you'll read about one later in this chapter!), but that was the first time in my life I thought we were going down. All I could do was grab Jack's hand and start praying out loud. When Jack started praying out loud, it really scared me because then I knew that he was worried too! In fact, it was evident that *everyone* on the flight was scared.

What made the experience even more frightening, however, was that there were no announcements from the cockpit—not "Ladies and gentlemen, we've entered a storm and it's going to be very rough for the next few minutes" or "Please bear with us and we'll get you through"—not even "Please return to your seats and keep your seat belts fastened." I'm used to pilots on U.S. airlines who keep passengers updated during the flight, but we heard NOTHING. The silence made me think, *Oh, no! They're scared too!*

Finally, the shaking stopped, and the plane resumed a normal pattern. Adrenaline was running so high that we all spent the rest of the trip awake and talking, even though we were flying through the night. The moment the wheels touched down in Los Angeles, everyone on the plane burst into spontaneous applause.

I was struck by how much it would have helped to hear a few words of comfort from the cockpit. We can bear a great deal of physical discomfort if it is tempered by emotional comfort—the assurance that someone else knows what is happening and is in a position to help us get through it. How fortunate we are that as our journey takes us through what is fearful and uncertain, we may rely on the comforting presence of our heavenly Father. He is "the Father of mercies and God of all comfort" (2 Cor. 1:3 NASB).

"Can you recall a time when God comforted you in the midst of a fearful experience?"

God Sees Us

Why is my mistress treating me so cruelly? After all, it wasn't my idea that I should become pregnant by Abram. How can I ever go back to that household again and put up with Sarai's jealousy and harshness, day after day after day? Perhaps I ridiculed her a little too much, but after all, I'm the one who's going to have the baby—something Sarai has never experienced! The only thing left for me to do is run away—go back to Egypt.

Wait—what is this? A voice? An *angel*?

The angel [of the LORD] said to her, "Hagar, Sarai's servant, where have you come from, and where are you going?" "I am running away from my mistress," she replied. Then the angel of the LORD said, "Return to your mistress and submit to her authority. . . . I will give you more descendants than you can count. . . . You are now pregnant and will give birth to a son. You are to name him Ishmael, for the LORD has heard about your misery. . . ." Thereafter, Hagar referred to the LORD, who had spoken to her, as "the God who sees me. . . . I have seen the One who sees me!" (Gen. 16:8–11, 13 NLT)

A mistreated, lonely, "used" servant fled from the heartache and pain that had become her way of life. On the road she encountered the angel of the Lord, who intercepted the young woman in her distress. He gave her guidance on what to do, granted her a promise for the future, and assured her that God was not blind to her pain. What a picture of God's comforting presence!

Outwardly, nothing changed in her life, but inwardly, she had been comforted by the God of all comfort. This reality can make all the difference in how we live.

I think what impresses me most about this remarkable meeting is Hagar's response. She had been told to return and submit to Sarai— go back to your hard circumstances and stay there. That was not exactly good news, but there is no record that Hagar resisted or argued with the Lord. The response from her we witness was, "God sees me. He cares about me. He knows about me and my affliction. I have seen God!" Her eyes were no longer focused on her situation; they were focused on God.

If God knew about her misery, Hagar could endure her difficult circumstances. It was enough. Outwardly, nothing changed in her life, but inwardly, she had been comforted by the God of all comfort. This reality can make all the difference in how we live.

183

Some years ago I was struggling with a difficult situation. Even after much prayer it seemed that there was no good resolution possible for these circumstances. I began to listen more intently to the Lord, and He whispered in my heart, *Cynthia, I am with you in this. I care about you and the person you care about. I know what you are going through. I see you.* I wanted the Lord to go on and say, *Now . . . this is what is going to happen.* But there was only the assurance that He saw my pain. It was His comfort for me, and it was enough.

—————

"Are you experiencing the comfort
of knowing that God sees your distress?"

—————

God Is
with Us

In the book of Isaiah, we receive an incredible promise, filled with comfort:

> When you pass through the waters, I will be with you;
> And through the rivers, they will not overflow you.
> When you walk through the fire, you will not be scorched,
> Nor will the flame burn you.
> For I am the LORD your God,
> The Holy One of Israel, your Savior. (43:2–3 NASB)

We are not exempt from trials, but we are never alone in them. We could ask Shadrach, Meshach, and Abednego if this promise is true. Can you go through fire without being burned? Will God be with you? I think their testimony would strengthen us to walk through our trials in the assurance that we are not left to endure alone.

❧

It was an extremely windy day, and I was flying from Washington, D.C., to Philadelphia. I didn't realize that I would be on a small plane until they called our flight and loaded all thirteen of us on a shuttle to take us out to the tarmac where our plane awaited us.

All of us were silent as we faced each other across the minibus. The atmosphere made me feel as if I were being taken to a concentration camp. Finally, an elderly man seated next to me said, "It sure is windy today, isn't it?"

"Yes," I agreed, "and I don't like to fly when it's so windy, especially in a small plane."

"Well," he replied, "I think we'll be just fine. We don't have anything to worry about."

"I certainly hope so!" I responded.

We climbed onto the plane, and I noticed that the little white bags were prominently displayed in the seat pockets. As I took my seat near the front, the flight attendant informed us that due to the roughness of flight, there would be no beverage service. Also, she said, we needed to fasten our seat belts tightly because of the coming turbulence. She suggested that anyone who so desired could change seats and move toward the front of the plane where it might be a *little* less bumpy.

The older gentleman I had spoken with in the shuttle came forward and sat across the aisle from me. He smiled and said, "It should be a little less bumpy up here."

Again, I replied, "I hope so!"

The pilot then came on the speaker: "Ladies and gentlemen, there is not smooth altitude up there. Tighten your belts, and I'll get you there as best I can."

Apprehension and dread filled my heart. *Lord,* I prayed, *I think I'd rather be having a root canal right now than be on this flight.*

As we took off, the man across from me gave me a big, reassuring smile.

In my extensive flight experience, I would definitely award that trip a close second to my trans-Pacific adventure for "roughest flight ever experienced" (at least the plane to Philadelphia didn't sound like it was about to fall apart). I kept my eyes closed as much as possible and prayed for two things: that our plane would land safely, and that my food would stay down.

Occasionally, I glanced around the plane. Most of the people were sick or keeping their eyes closed. Every time I looked across the aisle, the man who had befriended me was serenely reading a magazine! He always smiled at me.

When we landed, he said brightly, "Well, we made it, didn't we?"

We chatted briefly as the plane came to a stop, and then he climbed down the stairway to get his luggage. I was the last one off the plane, and as I stood at the top of the stairs watching our little group claim their bags, my eyes fell on this man who had been by my side throughout this trying experience. As I looked at him, the Lord whispered in my heart, *Cynthia, that was My man chosen to accompany you on this flight. He was with you to comfort you.* At the doorway of the plane, I wept unashamedly.

Whether that man was an angel or just someone God used in a special way, I don't know. All I know is that my Lord knew of my circumstances, and He was *with* me. God allowed me to go through the trial, but He did not leave me to go through it alone. He was with me to comfort me. The words of the hymn are true: "Be still, my soul! The Lord is on thy side. . . . Leave to thy God to order and provide."

━━━━━

"As you go through trials, can you rest in the Lord and trust Him to order and provide comfort for you?"

━━━━━

God Comforts Others Through Us

Paul tells us that God's comfort does not stop with us: "He comforts us in all our troubles so that we can comfort others. When others are troubled, we will be able to give them the same comfort God has given us" (2 Cor. 1:4 NLT).

> *It is reassuring to hear someone say, "I know how you feel."*

A friend of mine endured a deep tragedy. She needed to talk to another woman who had been through the same experience. Her question was, "Is the pain always this intense?" Through a support-group network, she was able to connect with someone who had suffered in a similar way. The response she received was, "No, the pain will not always be this severe, but it will always be there." That was a comfort to my friend, and she knew this person spoke the truth because the woman had lived for fifteen years with her sorrow.

It is reassuring to hear someone say, "I know how you feel." The words of a friend who has firsthand experience of your pain have incredible power to comfort.

At a conference where I was speaking, a woman sought me out to speak with me. With a heavy heart, she explained her situation. I was amazed—her story was my story. When she finished, I said, "You have come to someone who can totally identify with what you are going through and how you feel." My words had credibility, for she knew I understood her anguish. I was able to console this friend, for I had received solace from the Lord. I shared how God had led me to respond to the circumstances. I was able to say to her with confidence that God would be with her, that He saw her pain, and that His strength was sufficient. She left encouraged because she had been comforted by someone who had been comforted by the Lord.

To see God redeem our trials and use them in others' lives gives meaning and hope to our suffering. Those who have suffered and received God's comfort are real. They are approachable. They do not have all the answers, but they know the One who does. They know that God will somehow cause all of our pain to work for good, and that in the midst of His sovereign work, He will support and sustain us. He is a redeeming God who sees, who is with us, and who gifts us with a ministry of consolation. His comfort becomes our comfort for others.

Oswald Chambers commented that suffering has a unique power to strengthen us for giving to others:

> Suffering either gives me my self or it destroys my self. . . . You
> always know the man who has been through the fires of sorrow
> and received himself, you are certain you can go to him in trouble
> and find that he has ample leisure for you. If a man has not been
> through the fires of sorrow, he is apt to be contemptuous, he has

no time for you. If you receive yourself in the fires of sorrow, God will make you nourishment for other people.[2]

"What opportunities do you have for comforting others?"

Our Comfort Equals Our Suffering

Paul gives us wonderful news: "For just as the sufferings of Christ are ours in abundance, so also our comfort is abundant through Christ" (2 Cor. 1:5 NASB).

I have read this verse many times on my journey, but it wasn't until recently that I saw that our comfort is given in proportion to our affliction. When I am anxious about a tight schedule, I need the comfort of God's Word in my heart. When I take turbulent flights, God sends a messenger. When I am in deep distress, He becomes to me "the God who sees."

Job's life was an excellent example of enduring abundant suffering and receiving abundant comfort. Job's affliction had been catastrophic. He anguished as one who felt that his suffering was far too much for him to bear. And God was silent.

Where do we turn when we don't sense God's comfort at the time? I think we do what Job did. He cried out to God,

> I cry to you, O God, but you don't answer me. I stand before you, and you don't bother to look. You have become cruel toward me. You persecute me with your great power. You throw me into the whirlwind and destroy me in the storm. (Job 30:20–22 NLT)

After Job cried out to God, the abundant comfort came. His greatest comfort was seeing God and having his relationship radically changed by his firsthand encounter with the God of the universe. Job's brothers and sisters and friends came to him and consoled him and brought generous gifts, but God restored his fortune and then doubled it:

> GOD blessed Job's later life even more than his earlier life. He ended up with fourteen thousand sheep, six thousand camels, one

thousand teams of oxen, and one thousand donkeys. He also had
seven sons and three daughters. He named the first daughter
Dove, the second, Cinnamon, and the third, Darkeyes. There was
not a woman in that country as beautiful as Job's daughters. Their
father treated them as equals with their brothers, providing the
same inheritance. . . . Job lived on another hundred and forty
years, living to see his children and grandchildren—four genera-
tions of them! Then he died—an old man, a full life.
(Job 42:12–17 *The Message*)

King David suffered deep affliction as well. Listen to his response
when he had been deeply hurt by a beloved friend:

I call to GOD;
   GOD will help me.
At dusk, dawn, and noon I sigh
   deep sighs—he hears, he rescues. . . .
And this, my best friend, betrayed his best friends;
   his life betrayed his word.
All my life I've been charmed by his speech,
   never dreaming he'd turn on me.
His words, which were music to my ears,
   turned to daggers in my heart.
Pile your troubles on GOD's shoulders—
   he'll carry your load, he'll help you out.
   (Ps. 55:16–17, 20–22 *The Message*)

In their suffering, both Job and David poured out their hearts to God.
Job was devastated by the Lord Himself; David was in anguish over a
friend. Whatever our turmoil, God wants us to release our feelings to
Him. The very act of verbalizing our pain and casting our anxiety upon
Him will open our hearts to receive His comfort. The psalmist tells us
how: "O my people, trust in him at all times. / Pour out your heart to
him, for God is our refuge" (Ps. 62:8 NLT).

Hagar tells us that God sees us in our affliction. Shadrach, Meshach,
and Abednego demonstrate that God is with us in our trials. Job testifies

that God's comfort is abundant. David sings that God rescues and is our refuge. Here is a small cloud of witnesses to God's comfort. When you feel hopeless, you can remember their testimonies and be encouraged that your God is the God of all comfort.

I received a beautiful testimony from a precious young woman who suffered the death of her young son through sudden infant death syndrome (SIDS). Here is an excerpt from her letter:

> I never did get really angry with God, for God held up his end of the bargain. He blessed us with a loving son to raise in HIS will. I just was not prepared for what his will was to bring or how much this trial would hurt. So I started praying daily, and daily I would walk and pray, pray and walk. One day I was exceptionally hurt that someone who had been through the loss of a child through SIDS was not calling me. I was telling God how much it hurt and I needed to talk to someone who had been through this. He ever so gently said, "Then come to me for I lost my son also." I had never had such a prayerful experience in my life and was so awestruck I had to sit down. God answered me like he was standing right there. And that's when it finally hit me, God is here, he is walking with me, but most importantly he is ALIVE.[3]

This is the heart of the Father toward whom you journey: "In all their suffering he also suffered, and he personally rescued them. In his love and mercy he redeemed them. He lifted them up and carried them through all the years" (Isa. 63:9 NLT).

> *Never a trial that He is not there,*
> *Never a burden that He doth not bear,*
> *Never a sorrow that He doth not share,*
> *Moment by moment, I'm under His care.*[4]

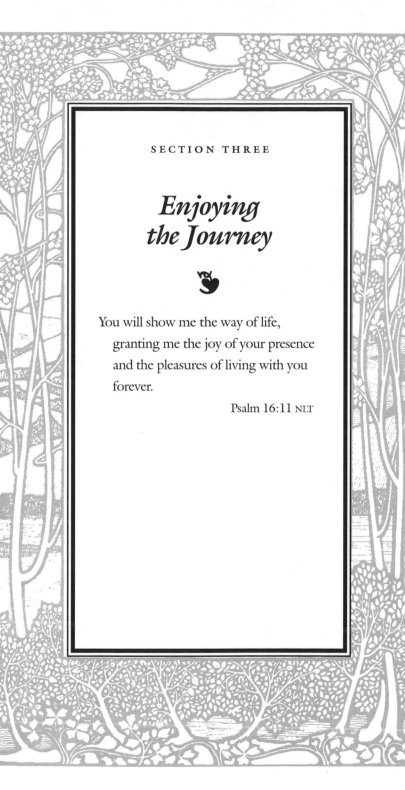

SECTION THREE

Enjoying the Journey

You will show me the way of life,
    granting me the joy of your presence
    and the pleasures of living with you
    forever.

Psalm 16:11 NLT

The Father
and the Child

The Father spoke:

And what do you know of My heart?

I know that Your heart is the only worthy
destination.

How have you learned this truth?

By walking daily with You.

How are your companions, Joy and Sorrow?

Now that I have a better understanding of Your
heart, I realize that Sorrow keeps me dependent upon
You and Joy enables me to stay on the journey.

You have learned well, My child. So you wish to
continue the journey?

Oh, Father, I only pray that I remain faithful and obe-
dient. I want no other journey—I seek no other Joy.

You will find Joy in loving and serving others.

It is hard for me to love and serve. How can I do it
with Joy?

By taking My yoke and learning of Me.

As long as I am yoked to You, Father, I know I can do
anything.

Hold My hand tightly, My child. For this part of
the journey, you must receive My rest and learn
to live for all that is eternal.

Why must I hold Your hand tightly?

Because I am ready to place you as a laborer in
My harvest, and I do not want you to be so busy in
your service that you loosen your grip or let go.

And how do I labor in Your harvest?

By bringing Me glory.

TWENTY

Bearing His Fruit

We mostly spend those lives conjugating three verbs: to Want, to Have and to Do. Craving, clutching, and fussing, on the material, political, social, emotional, intellectual—even on the religious—plane, we are kept in perpetual unrest: forgetting that none of these verbs have any ultimate significance, except so far as they are transcended by and included in, the fundamental verb, to Be: and that Being, not wanting, having and doing, is the essence of the spiritual life.

Evelyn Underhill[1]

I find that after spending a length of time with someone, I tend to begin copying the other person's mannerisms and even the accent. I am originally from Texas, but I haven't lived there for twenty years. I've noticed, though, that whenever I travel to East Texas and spend time with friends, I come back to Arizona with a more distinct Texas twang!

We do tend to pick up each other's characteristics. After traveling with our Guide over the years, by His grace we will begin to imitate His character and heart. Years of staying on the journey with Him, day by day, will slowly but surely begin to produce the fruit of the Spirit in our lives.

This is just as He planned—live with Me, walk with Me, stay close to Me, and you will bear the fruit of My Spirit.

Bearing Fruit for the Church

"But when the Holy Spirit controls our lives," Paul tells us, "he will produce this kind of fruit in us: love, joy, peace, patience, kindness, goodness, faithfulness, gentleness, and self-control" (Gal. 5:22–23 NLT).

Years of staying on the journey with Him, day by day, will slowly but surely begin to produce the fruit of the Spirit in our lives.

When we are consistently walking with the Lord and allowing the Holy Spirit to control us, precious fruit will be produced. This happens as we understand that Jesus is the Vine, and we are the branches. A branch must stay connected to the Vine if it is to bear fruit. And that is *all* the branch has to do! As we stay joined to the Lord, His life will begin to flow through us. In that living union, our inner *being* gives rise to our *doing*.

Jesus gave His disciples a new commandment: "Love each other. Just as I have loved you, you should love each other. Your love for one another will prove to the world that you are my disciples" (John 13:34–35 NLT). The second-century Roman emperor Hadrian received a report on the behavior of the early Christians that described them as follows:

> They love one another. They never fail to help widows; they save orphans from those who would hurt them. If they have something they give freely to the man who has nothing; if they see a stranger, they take him home, and are happy, as though he were a real brother. They don't consider themselves brothers in the usual sense, but brothers instead through the Spirit, in God.[2]

The Christians' vibrant love for one another was a living testimony to the world that they were Christ's disciples. Our fruit needs to be evident—not just seen, but demonstrated in a lifestyle. Genuine love is not something we can put at the top of our to-do list and then check off when we have accomplished it. It is a characteristic that wells up from our lives authentically and spontaneously. This kind of love is eloquently described in 1 Corinthians 13:

> Love is patient and kind. Love is not jealous or boastful or proud
> or rude. Love does not demand its own way. Love is not irritable,
> and it keeps no record of when it has been wronged. It is never
> glad about injustice but rejoices whenever the truth wins out.
> Love never gives up, never loses faith, is always hopeful, and
> endures through every circumstance. (vv. 4–7 NLT)

This concise exposition of love speaks more of love's character and less of specific acts. Love expresses itself in action, but these qualities must be taking root and growing in our hearts before we act, for then it is God's love that is exhibited, not our own.

"Where have you witnessed the Christian community bearing fruit in love for one another?"

From the flow of Christ's life within us, we will bear fruit that manifests itself in good works. "Dear children, let us stop just saying we love each other," wrote the apostle John. "Let us really show it by our actions" (1 John 3:18 NLT). It is recorded of Tabitha that "she was always doing kind things for others and helping the poor" (Acts 9:36 NLT). Priscilla and Aquila took the time to teach Apollos the way of God more accurately. There are many ways we can bear fruit among the household of faith—sewing, cooking, teaching, being patient, being undemanding, gently restoring a sister who has strayed from the path, sharing burdens, praying. As we journey, our fruit needs to nourish our fellow travelers, for this is the way that others will know we are Christ's disciples.

As we stay joined to the Lord, His life will begin to flow through us. In that living union, our inner being gives rise to our doing.

Bearing Fruit
for My Neighbor

The man was half dead. He had been robbed of his money and clothes, and then he had been severely beaten. Fortunately, someone from the nearby church came down the road. But when he saw him, he walked quickly away on the other side of the road from the tragic sight.

Then a church assistant came by, glanced at the man, and decided it was best not to get involved.

A third man came down the road, and it seemed likely that he would be no different from the first two. Besides, he wasn't even from that community. He was an outcast, a member of another race with whom the local church people had little contact—in fact, they deliberately avoided going anywhere near "those people."

> *As we journey, our fruit needs to nourish our fellow travelers, for this is the way that others will know we are Christ's disciples.*

But the third man did not walk past the victim lying by the side of the road. Instead, he stopped, dressed the man's wounds, put him on his donkey, and took him to an inn. He got him settled, stayed the night with him, and left him in the care of the innkeeper. Before leaving, the outcast covered the expenses and promised to pay any remaining bills when he returned.

Jesus told this parable in response to a religious scholar who asked the question, "What must I do to receive eternal life?" Jesus asked him what the Law of Moses said.

"Love God wholeheartedly and love your neighbor as yourself," the scholar replied.

Then Jesus said, "Do this, and you will live."

The scholar, however, wishing to justify himself, asked, "Who is my neighbor?"

As His answer, Jesus told the story of the good Samaritan.

This story is a remarkable answer, for it cuts through prejudice and social roles to define love practically. It provides several key guidelines for discerning how to meet a multitude of needs in today's world.

First, Jesus' parable teaches that *loving my neighbor is helping anyone who crosses my path and is in need.* The good Samaritan was not on a mission to minister to people. He was traveling to keep an appointment. It was "as he was going" that he helped this man.

This is helpful to me because it means I don't necessarily have to make elaborate plans to serve others. I just need to be alert to the needs of people I encounter as I go about my everyday life.

"Where does God give you opportunity to bear fruit in good works for your 'neighbor'?"

One day I was in the grocery store, hurrying to squeeze an errand into my commitments for that day, and I met an acquaintance. We visited briefly, and I was ready to say good-bye and finish my shopping. But there was something about her countenance that made me ask a more personal, "How are things going?" question. She shared a heartache, and I listened to her and offered comfort. I didn't really have the time, but I felt the Lord prompting me to draw her out and listen to her. I had met a neighbor who was in my path and in need.

Eugene Peterson describes this mode of bearing fruit for our neighbor as a kind of freedom:

> When we are free in Christ we are free to respond to the opportunities readily at hand for living the gospel in acts of "doing good." . . . We are free from anxiously watching out for the big chance for ourselves and thus free to respond to any chance encounters with the people we meet. We are free from the compulsion to always look good in front of others and thus free to do demeaning or embarrassing things in helping others. We live opportunity-alert.[3]

A second guideline to draw from this parable is, *loving my neighbor includes allowing other people to help.* The good Samaritan rescued the beaten man, but he trusted the innkeeper to look after him too. So often when I get involved with a person who is hurting or in need physically, I tend to take full responsibility for her, and it can become too much for me. It is a wise idea to ask others to help. The needy person gains other people she can relate to and the opportunity to benefit from their unique ministry gifts.

Third, I can affirm from Jesus' story that *loving my neighbor necessitates keeping my priorities.* The good Samaritan did all that he could for the injured man, yet he continued on his journey to keep his commitments.

> *I don't necessarily have to make elaborate plans to serve others. I just need to be alert to the needs of people I encounter as I go about my everyday life.*

As I look back on my life, I realize that in my zeal to help others, I too easily slighted my family because I was emotionally drained or physically fatigued. Not only that, but I tended to neglect my time with the Lord. My days became rushed, and I became stressed. This experience convinced me that it is important to ask others to help and to remain committed to keeping my priorities.

God's love flows into our lives as we remain a branch connected to the Vine. I want to bear the fruit of His love—not my human, self-serving, "let me save you" kind of love. That's why I like the good Samaritan. His goodness flowed naturally out of his life. He saw a need, met it as best he could, and felt free to honor his other responsibilities.

Fourth, this story teaches me that *loving my neighbor means loving whoever is in my path.* The good Samaritan knew that the hurting man was of a race who shunned his kind (the Jews scorned the Samaritans for their mixed, Jewish-Gentile ancestry), but he did not let that keep him from helping. He did not discriminate in reaching out to *whoever* was in need. Listen to Jesus drive this point home in His words in Matthew 5:43–48:

> You're familiar with the old written law, "Love your friend," and its unwritten companion, "Hate your enemy." I'm challenging that. I'm telling you to love your enemies. Let them bring out the best in you, not the worst. When someone gives you a hard time, respond with the energies of prayer, for then you are working out of your true selves, your God-created selves. This is what God does. He gives his best—the sun to warm and the rain to

nourish—to everyone, regardless: the good and bad, the nice and nasty. If all you do is love the lovable, do you expect a bonus? Anybody can do that. If you simply say hello to those who greet you, do you expect a medal? Any run-of-the-mill sinner does that. In a word, what I'm saying is, *Grow up*. You're kingdom subjects. Now live like it. Live out your God-created identity. Live generously and graciously toward others, the way God lives toward you. (*The Message*)

The Samaritan's love for his neighbor was expressed in extending care for a wounded man. Demanding as it is to meet someone's physical needs, however, it may be even more difficult to attend to some individuals' emotional needs. I can cook, bandage, and take pretty good care of someone physically, but what about a neighbor's child who is unruly, what about an abrasive neighbor, what about a demanding coworker, what about a family member who has hurt me, what about a Christian friend who is no longer a friend? How do I love when there is a barrier to helping someone? How do I love when it is hard to love my neighbor?

That's just the point—on my own, I can't love my difficult neighbor the way God commands. I must abide in Him, drawing love from the Vine, so I can share it with others. I love because I am loved. I obey His command to love my neighbor because it is my way of showing God that I love Him. I forgive because I have been forgiven. I seek to be patient, kind, and gracious because that is what love does. I seek to love in His strength because whatever I do without love is of no value.

Oswald Chambers commented, "This abandon to the love of Christ is the one thing that bears fruit in the life, and it will always leave the impression of the holiness and of the power of God, never of our personal holiness."[4]

"How would you describe the difference between loving in your own strength and loving in God's strength?"

Sharing
the Good News

Peter indicates that as we bear fruit in doing good to others, it will attract attention: "Through thick and thin, keep your hearts at attention, in adoration before Christ, your Master. Be ready to speak up and tell anyone who asks why you're living the way you are, and always with the utmost courtesy" (1 Peter 3:14–15 *The Message*).

Our love for our neighbor should prompt questions about why we are patient, why we don't lash back in anger, why we don't push for recognition, why we would take time to help. When this happens, we must always be ready to share the good news of the gospel gently and respectfully.

> *I want to bear the fruit of His love—not my human, self-serving, "let me save you" kind of love.*

I remember being asked on different occasions how I coped with three small children. Early in my Christian life I responded with a smile and said something lame such as, "Oh, I just take one day at a time." How I wish I had said, "Oh, it's because of my relationship with Jesus Christ!" This is what I do now. Whenever anyone sincerely asks, I gently and respectfully answer with the truth.

The principle here is that we should be Christ's ambassadors wherever we are, always alert to sharing the gospel. When my husband, Jack, has taken the initiative to help someone, he tells the person, "I'm so insensitive that if I did not have Jesus Christ as my personal Savior, I probably wouldn't have noticed that you needed help!"

Our privilege is to say with Paul, "For I am not ashamed of this Good News about Christ. It is the power of God at work, saving everyone who believes—Jews first and also Gentiles" (Rom. 1:16 NLT).

This testimony becomes a natural outflow of our walk of faith. If I've been to a really unique place or met a very special person, I can't wait to tell others about my experience. If we are enjoying our journey with the Lord, we want to tell others about what we have discovered.

Richard Halverson described this way of bearing fruit when he wrote,

For the New Testament Christians, witness was not a sales pitch. They simply shared, each in his own way, what they had received.

Theirs was not a formally prepared, carefully worked-out presentation with a gimmick to manipulate conversation, and a "closer" for an on-the-spot decision . . . but the spontaneous, irrepressible, effervescent enthusiasm of those who had met the most fascinating Person who ever lived. The gospel is not theology. It's a Person. Theology doesn't save. Jesus Christ saves. The first century disciples were followers of Jesus. They were filled with Jesus.[5]

As we begin to love our neighbor as ourselves, we will naturally be alert to opportunities for sharing the overflow of God's love in our lives. One night Jack and I ran an errand to an auto supply store to pick up a part for our car. Out in the parking lot was a young man working on his automobile. Jack went over to see if he could help. While they visited, Jack was able to share God's love with him. As a result, he received Christ, and he and his family have become like our children.

As you draw closer to God's heart, His fruit will become more evident in your life. In the words of John the Baptist, *He must increase, and you must decrease*. Your love for others will increasingly become an overflow of your abiding as you allow the Holy Spirit to reign in your life. Set your desire just to *be* with the Lord. For *being* who God wants you to be enables God to use you as He pleases in the lives of others. Your bearing fruit brings glory to God, builds the body of Christ, and brings others to the Savior. Your fruit is evidence of your journey to the heart of God, and it will bring you much joy in the Lord.

> *Redeemed—how I love to proclaim it!*
> *Redeemed by the blood of the Lamb;*
> *Redeemed through His infinite mercy,*
> *His child, and forever I am.*[6]

TWENTY-ONE

Experiencing His Rest

Instead of the word "submission" . . . I should write *acceptance,* for more and more, as life goes on, that word opens doors into rooms of infinite peace, and the heart that accepts asks nothing, for it is at rest, and the pilgrim of love does not need a map or chart: "I know my road, it leadeth to His heart."

Amy Carmichael[1]

Upon landing in Asia for an extended visit, we felt exhausted by the thirty-six-hour flight in four stages that had been required to get us there. Our hosts, eager to entertain us in their tradition of attentive hospitality, greeted us enthusiastically and took us immediately to a circus. The engrossing acts could not compete with our fatigue, however, and so most of us fell asleep! Perceiving that we were sorely in need of rest, the guide took us back early to the hotel.

Overseas tours create opportunities to get away from our daily routines, to see new wonders, and to explore different cultures. Most itineraries are filled with traveling to various sights, walking around a lot, taking pictures, packing and unpacking. Sometimes the schedule can be demanding. Few of us return from extended trips feeling rested and relaxed.

Many of my friends have remarked that taking a cruise is a much more relaxing way to travel, and they return feeling rejuvenated. An ocean voyage offers rest and refreshment *as* you go. When you disembark at the next port, you are ready to expend some energy.

> *The other night as I fell thankfully into bed, I thought about a T-shirt I'd seen with the saying, "I am woman. I am invincible. I am tired."*

I think we can view our journey with the Lord as though we are going on a cruise. He wants us to enjoy our journey and to experience continual renewal as we travel. This means that we need regular times of replenishment to be strengthened for the different ports to which He leads us. Our journey will extend for a lifetime, not just a season. It's important that we learn how to experience, along the way, the rest that only God can provide.

The psalmist provides a lovely picture of the rest that God makes possible, even in the midst of busy and hectic lives:

> The LORD is my shepherd;
> I have everything I need.
> He lets me rest in green meadows;
> he leads me beside peaceful streams.
> He renews my strength.
> He guides me along right paths,
> bringing honor to his name. (Ps. 23:1–3 NLT)

A Sabbath Rest

I don't know about you, but I find more often than not that the high point of my day is going to bed at night! I've wondered if there's a message in there for me, but many times I am busy because I need to be and there's no good way around it. The other night as I fell thankfully into bed, I thought about a T-shirt I'd seen with the saying, "I am woman. I am invincible. I am tired." I know that many other women join me in feeling the need to experience the Lord's rest while we continue on His journey.

From the beginning of creation, God has been concerned about rest for His children. It is so important that He instituted it in His Law as one of the Ten Commandments: "Remember to observe the Sabbath day by keeping it holy. Six days a week are set apart for your daily duties and regular work, but the seventh day is a day of rest dedicated to the LORD your God" (Ex. 20:8–10 NLT). The word *Sabbath* means "rest." This is a day to remember the Lord and to honor Him. It is a day for taking a break from work and enjoying a time of refreshment. In the rhythm of our lives, we need one day out of seven to stop, be still, worship, and be renewed spiritually and physically.

> *How can we turn down an invitation to trade in a heavy burden for a light load?*

As much as possible, Sunday is a day of rest for me. Going to worship on Sunday morning, having a leisurely afternoon of reading and resting, and enjoying pancakes for dinner is our usual routine for the Sabbath. It is a good way to get ready for tackling another six days.

I love Jesus' words to the Pharisees when they rebuked Him for letting His disciples break off heads of wheat on the Sabbath: "The Sabbath was made to benefit people," He admonished them, "and not people to benefit the Sabbath" (Mark 2:27 NLT). Resting one day a week is not a legalism to placate God, but a gift from Him for our benefit. It pleases Him when we accept and enjoy it as He intended.

"What does a restful Sunday look like for you?"

A Restful Yoke

Jesus' words in Matthew 11:28–30 reveal that our need for rest has a special place in God's heart: "Come to me, all of you who are weary and carry heavy burdens, and I will give you rest. Take my yoke upon you. Let me teach you, because I am humble and gentle, and you will find rest for your souls. For my yoke fits perfectly, and the burden I give you is light" (NLT).

Imagine that you receive a special invitation in the mail. You open the envelope, pull out the card, and read:

To All Who Are Weary and Heavy-Laden:
You are cordially invited to receive
Rest and Teaching
accompanied by
Humility and Gentleness.
Complimentary, personalized yokes* will be given to all who come.
*Yokes: sized perfectly and guaranteed to be light. Continual instruction provided personally by the Creator.

To receive an invitation to come to Jesus and be yoked to Him—joined, connected, united, coupled, attached—is humbling. That He wants us continually by His side is a wonderful sign of His love for us.

How can we turn down an invitation to trade in a heavy burden for a light load? To be taught by the Master Teacher who is humble and gentle is a high privilege. To be yoked to our Lord and Savior is a supreme honor. The way of living that this relationship offers is refreshing. It is quiet and calm. It is comforting and restoring. It is restful because the Prince of Peace is in the yoke with us.

What are the benefits of being yoked with the Lord? Here is a list I can testify to firsthand. I encourage you to add to it from your own experience.

- I hear His voice.
- He sets my pace.
- He guides me.
- He instructs me.
- He helps me to carry the load.
- He gives me peace.
- He never leaves me.
- He gives me rest.

"Are you experiencing the benefits of being
yoked with the Lord?"

And how do we become yoked with the Lord? I recommend the following steps:

- Come to Him.
- Relinquish control.
- Accept His will for you.
- Give Him permission to be Lord of your life.
- Walk with Him.
- Stay with Him.

I accepted the Lord's invitation to wear His yoke the afternoon I relinquished control of my life. None of the circumstances of my life changed, but I immediately began to experience His rest. Because of this rest, I knew I could continue with my life as it was. I also began to know the Lord's guidance and instruction in fresh ways. I was more attentive to the Scriptures and to His voice because I had put on His yoke.

Ruth, the Moabite, accepted His yoke also. He guided her to Bethlehem and to the field of Boaz. She willingly wore His yoke as she worked in the harvest and served her mother-in-law. She wore it well, for her reputation was one of being a woman of honor and excellence. She let the Lord lead her, and as a result, she experienced His peace in the midst of her less-than-desirable circumstances. She found her rest by seeking refuge under the shelter of His wings.

The Abiding Servant
Versus
the Busy Servant

Being yoked to the Lord is a beautiful picture of abiding in Him. One of the very practical benefits of this partnership is that we can allow Him to set the pace for our journey. As we abide, we receive instruction concerning how He wants us to serve Him—what "ports" He wants us to visit and how long we are to dwell there.

We have explored how Mary of Bethany was intent on abiding with the Lord and how her service overflowed from it. Because she sat at His feet, she wanted to express her love for Him by anointing His body for burial. She depicts the abiding servant.

Martha represents the busy servant. She loved the Lord, but in her serving she became anxious and bothered. She was not at *rest*. Everything she did was in some sense a chore, and chores can easily become burdens. Since her identity came from her service, she had little time to sit at the feet of Jesus. She had stepped out of her Lord's yoke.

If we are consistently joined to the Lord, we will seek His guidance before accepting any additions to our schedule or any commitments to serve. His desire is to give us rest and burdens that are light. This doesn't mean that we are not busy, but it does mean that in our God-directed busyness, His strength and grace are with us.

―――

*"Do you ever experience the Lord's rest
in the midst of your busyness?"*

―――

Several of my friends frequently comment that they could not keep my schedule. As I have listened to them, I've thought that I could not serve as they are serving. Two of my good friends have ministered to their dying mothers-in-law in their own homes. I think this is an incredible service to the Lord. I don't know that I would have the patience necessary to serve in this way. But this is my point—when our service is the will of God, we have His power to do what He gives us to do. We experience His refreshment in the process of our work that is done for Him.

Where do you suppose Jesus wanted Martha the day He visited her home—in the kitchen, or at His feet? I think He desired her to be at His feet. If Martha had as much as a crust of bread and a fish or two, then they were in good shape for a meal. The Lord was there, and He provides all that we need, including rest.

Oswald Chambers commented on our need to be dependent upon God in our serving:

> Most of us live on the borders of consciousness—consciously serving, consciously devoted to God. All this is immature, it is not the real life yet. The mature stage is the life of a child which is never conscious; we become so abandoned to God that the consciousness of being used never enters in. When we are consciously being used as broken bread and poured-out wine, there is another stage to be reached where all consciousness of ourselves and of what God is doing through us is eliminated. A saint is never consciously a saint; a saint is consciously dependent on God.[2]

Resting and Waiting

"Rest in the LORD and wait patiently for Him," we are told (Ps. 37:7 NASB). These are beautiful words, but they are extraordinarily hard to put into practice. I like the way Saint Jerome described it: "*'Hold thee still'* (so it may be translated). And this is the hardest precept that is given to man; insomuch that the most difficult precept of action sinks into nothing when compared with this command to inaction."[3]

The Lord wants us to trust Him with all our hearts, and part of that trust is resting and waiting for His timing. I am the epitome of impatience. I have always thought, for example, that seven months was long enough to be pregnant! Two-plus years was too long to have to change diapers. Four years was too long to be in that old house. Any delay in an airport is stressful. It is difficult to obey the command just to wait.

After Noah finished building the ark, God sent the animals and then instructed that Noah and his family should board the ark. Picture this: the whole family, with all the animals in the world, are ready to set sail. While I was reading the passage one day, I was amazed to realize that after everyone was safely aboard, it was *one week* before the flood came and covered the earth (Gen. 7:10). If I had been Mrs. Noah, I would have said, "Lord, we're ready to go. I've got everything arranged. I don't understand why we're all just sitting here now. Besides, it's embarrassing—our neighbors keep walking by and laughing at us. Lord, we only needed a day or two to get settled. Seven days are too long!"

Joseph had to learn to rest and wait on the Lord during the many long years that he was a slave and a prisoner.

> **Rest, refreshment, and renewal *are healing words. God wants to make them a reality in your life.***

David, who wrote the words *rest and wait,* had to wait almost fifteen years to become king after he was anointed for the position.

Esther learned to wait overnight before telling her husband about the decree that would destroy the Jews.

The prize for waiting, though, goes to Abraham and Sarah. They waited twenty-five years for the birth of Isaac after the good news was announced.

God has His time schedule, and He uses what we call delays to produce in us patience and trust, and to accomplish His purposes in establishing His kingdom. God delayed the rains of the Great Flood for a week to give others time to repent. Abraham and Sarah and everyone who knew them could give glory only to God for the gift of Isaac. Esther's appeal would not have had the desired effect on her husband had she not waited. In His sovereignty, God's timing is always perfect. Since His ways are not our ways, He wants us to *rest* in our waiting.

A. B. Davidson gives this definition of the value of waiting: "To wait is not merely to remain impassive. It is to expect—to look for with patience, and also with submission. It is to long for, but not impatiently; to look for, but not to fret at the delay; to watch for, but not restlessly."[4]

To those who *rest* (abide in Him) and *wait* (accept His will and timing), strength is given: "But those who wait on the LORD will find new strength. They will fly high on wings like eagles. They will run and not grow weary. They will walk and not faint" (Isa. 40:31 NLT). The eagle is a wonderfully descriptive image of the strength we draw from waiting.

"In what areas of your life is God teaching you to wait upon Him?"

A Psalm of Rest

The psalmist provides a beautiful picture of one who is at rest with her Lord in the image of a weaned child:

> LORD, my heart is not proud;
>   my eyes are not haughty.
> I don't concern myself with matters too great
>   or awesome for me.
> But I have stilled and quieted myself,
>   just as a small child is quiet with its mother.
> Yes, like a small child is my soul within me.
> O Israel, put your hope in the LORD—
>   now and always. (Ps. 131 NLT)

This psalm has always meant a lot to me. It speaks to me of humility, simplicity, and trust. The writer, David, takes responsibility for quieting himself before the Lord. He can be still because he is not constantly preoccupied with protecting his pride. He doesn't worry about things he can't understand. He just comes to his Lord and rests in His presence. Charles Spurgeon commented:

> It is one of the shortest Psalms to read, but one of the longest to learn. It speaks of a young child, but it contains the experience of a man in Christ. Lowliness and humility are here seen in connection with a sanctified heart, a will subdued to the mind of God, and a hope looking to the Lord alone. Happy is the man who can without falsehood use these words as his own; for he wears about him the likeness of his Lord, who said, "I am meek and lowly in heart."[5]

Rest, refreshment, and renewal are healing words. God wants to make them a reality in your life. The Lord Himself will provide everything you need, particularly rest and strength, for your daily walk. Green meadows and peaceful streams are part of your journey. Wear His yoke so that you allow Him to lead you there. Let Him set your pace and guide you to the right paths. Receive the freedom He offers you from having to worry about what lies ahead. Truly, the heart that accepts His will and guidance asks nothing. Abiding in Him provides the relationship that is the source of rest, discernment for service, strength, and the patience to wait and trust.

Green meadows and peaceful streams are part of your journey. Wear His yoke so that you allow Him to lead you there.

Perhaps this prayer will help you quiet yourself before the Lord:

Dear Lord, I know that without Your rest, I will not have strength for the journey, I will not enjoy the journey, and I will not bring You glory. I want to come to You and receive Your yoke, which enables me to receive Your rest and direction. I want to come before You in all honesty and say that my heart is not conceited and my eyes are not arrogant or pretentious. I don't want to be concerned about things that I can't understand; I want to trust You. I want to continue to grow so that I can come to You without demanding something in return. I want to know the joy and peace of Your presence. I want to be like a weaned child who asks for nothing. I want Your rest.

Hidden in the hollow
Of His blessed hand,
Never foe can follow,
Never traitor stand;
Not a surge of worry,
Not a shade of care,
Not a blast of hurry
Touch the spirit there.
Trusting in Jehovah,
Hearts are truly blest—
Finding, as He promised,
Perfect peace and rest.[6]

TWENTY-TWO

Living for the Eternal

In any case there is some point in not constructing one's happiness on the basis of consumption and prosperity alone. But in the light of Jesus Christ it also makes sense not to be always striving, not always to be trying to have everything; not to be governed by the laws of prestige and competition; not to take part in the cult of abundance.

Hans Küng[1]

S hopping has been included in just about every excursion I've been on. I enjoy shopping because I find it interesting to look for unique gifts and souvenirs. I have many material reminders scattered throughout my home that pleasantly remind me of different trips. As I look back over my travel, however, it's not the material things that stand out in my memory. Rather, I remember scenic wonders such as certain mountains and waterfalls, and I fondly recall the special people with whom we stayed.

One of my favorite places is Niagara Falls. I will never forget taking the boat to see the falls up close. The relatively small craft (the closer we got to the giant cascades, the smaller it became!) took us right under the churning wall of water, where we could fully appreciate its immensity and power. The force of the huge spray produced surging whirlpools that seemed to pull us into the falls. It was frightening and exhilarating all at the same time. I felt exceedingly insignificant as I stood in humble awe of God's creation and might. My glimpse of this small part of the Lord's handiwork will stay with me forever.

I have also been fortunate to stay in the homes of people in other countries who have generously opened their hearts and homes to me. I have been eternally influenced by their hospitality and friendship. In particular, I remember a family in New Zealand who took me in as if I were one of their own. They took me around the country and frequently went out of their way to make sure I was comfortable (at the time, that meant being warm enough!). I got to know the grandparents as well as each of the children, and they all made me feel very at home. They will always have a special place in my heart.

I find that the people I've met and the evidence of God's creative artistry mean much more to me than the souvenirs I bring home. This is as it should be. The closer we travel to the Lord's heart, the more we will focus on what is of lasting value. We will discover that the joy of the journey is closely bound up with living for the eternal.

The Temporary Versus the Eternal

"But as for me, how good it is to be near God!" Asaph wrote. "I have made the Sovereign LORD my shelter, and I will tell everyone about the wonderful things you do" (Ps. 73:28 NLT).

These are beautiful words, but before Asaph came to that conclusion, he struggled with some issues that we all face today. Listen to his honest admission:

> For I envied the proud
> when I saw them prosper despite their wickedness.
> They seem to live such a painless life;
> their bodies are so healthy and strong.

They aren't troubled like other people
    or plagued with problems like everyone else. (Ps. 73:3–5 NLT)

It sounds as if Asaph had been watching the *Lifestyles of the Rich and Famous*. It is hard to see the wicked prosper. They spend their lives in pursuit of bigger houses they can afford to redecorate. They have time to preoccupy themselves with exotic places and new adventures. Much of their money is spent on cultivating sleek, tanned bodies. They drive the newest cars. Expensive clothes and jewelry fill their ample closets. Parties and entertainment are the focus of their evenings and conversations.

Sounds like fun to me! I agree with Asaph: "But as for me, I came so close to the edge of the cliff! / My feet were slipping, and I was almost gone" (Ps. 73:2 NLT).

It is hard to stay on the path toward God when all the people who are headed in the opposite direction seem to be enjoying the good life. It is so easy to desire their abundance and seemingly carefree and glamorous lives.

But I find that it's not only the wicked I envy; I have trouble with the prosperity of the righteous! God loves to bless us, and He gives as He wills. It is perfectly right and good to be favored with riches, and I have several wonderful friends who love God and who have exquisite homes and furnishings. I enjoy the opportunity to visit with them in their lovely homes, but then I tend to have reentry problems when I come back to my house!

I visited one house that was so large, it would have been helpful to have a map to find my way around. Another home had a lovely indoor spa. One home I particularly loved had a sitting area, a fireplace, and a little library—all in the master bedroom. I have always wished for a cozy little area in our bedroom where Jack and I could have tea and leisurely visits. It would have been especially nice while we were living with four teenagers!

A dear friend had just built a new home, and she invited me over to see it. It was large and elegant. As we toured, she said, "Would you like to see the master closet? We just finished it." I have always admired walk-in closets. But this time I wanted to say, "Honestly, no thank you, because when I go home and see my little bifold door closet, I will be envious—and my feet will come close to slipping!"

To understand the difference between living for heaven and demanding that life here on earth be like heaven is an important lesson in learning to live for the eternal.

Comparison disturbs contentment. Anytime I begin to look at others and compare my life or possessions to theirs, I will most likely conclude that I have been treated unfairly. Amy Carmichael pictured our discontent as a mountain: "There is a mountain which, when I find myself compassing it, I call by this name, Discontent with the ways of God. It has other names which sound nicer, but I think this name strips it of all pretence."[2]

If I envy, and if I am discontent, it is because I am dissatisfied with God's provision for my perceived needs. My eyes are focused on what I have been denied, not on what I have been given. And it's all God's fault!

"Where are you most tempted to focus on the temporal over the eternal?"

I was in Houston to help my mom and visit with my dad, who was quite ill. After my stay, they took me to the airport. It was an emotional parting for me because I knew that my dad was not doing well. In fact, they were on their way to the doctor when they dropped me off.

As I walked up to the ticket counter, my heart sank, for I realized that in saying good-bye I had left my tickets in the backseat of the car. *Lord,* I cried out to Him, *I'm trying to do everything right. I've been here with my parents; I'm going home to be with Jack. In between, I'm serving You by speaking. It seems that You could at least remind me to get my tickets! Besides, I'm looking around and I see all these other people with their tickets—they're not having to do what I'm doing, but things are going smoothly for them! It's not fair!* I was saying with Asaph:

Was it for nothing that I kept my heart pure
and kept myself from doing wrong?

All I get is trouble all day long;
> every morning brings me pain. (Ps. 73:13–14 NLT)

I'm the one having the hassles. I'm the one with the small closet. I'm the one who, for years, drove our old car we aptly named "the gutless wonder." *It seems that there could be a few perks along the way, Lord, especially when just about all the people I know seem to have everything they need!* When I am in this state, I recall the words of Paul:

> This is the reason why we never lose heart. The outward man does indeed suffer wear and tear, but every day the inward man receives fresh strength. These little troubles (which are really so transitory) are winning for us a permanent, glorious and solid reward out of all proportion to our pain. For we are looking all the time not at the visible things but at the invisible. The visible things are transitory: it is the invisible things that are really permanent. (2 Cor. 4:16–18 PHILLIPS)

What a good reminder! We should not lose heart over our circumstances—for the visible is only temporary. God's interest is in our hearts and in all that is eternal. My desire is for everything to be perfect in my life. God's desire is to strengthen me in the midst of my imperfect circumstances so that I become the woman He wants me to be, where He has me. He wants me to learn to live for the invisible. Dan Allender writes,

> It seems that most of my life is sacrificed protecting and enhancing a home that is supposedly not my home. . . . How would you answer the questions, "Do I live for heaven?" or "Do I live demanding that life be like heaven?" Your answers will determine what you will spend your life fighting for.[3]

To understand the difference between living *for* heaven and demanding that life here on earth *be like* heaven is an important lesson in learning to live for the eternal. To begin to focus on the eternal rather than the temporary will make all the difference in our journey. Let's see how Asaph began to understand the principle:

> So I tried to understand why the wicked prosper.
> But what a difficult task it is!

Then one day I went into your sanctuary, O God,
    and I thought about the destiny of the wicked.
Truly, you put them on a slippery path
    and send them sliding over the cliff to destruction.
In an instant they are destroyed,
    swept away by terrors.
Their present life is only a dream
    that is gone when they awake. (Ps. 73:16–20 NLT)

As Asaph went before the Lord, he began to understand that in reality, life is like a dream that is over when morning comes. This life is only temporary! The wicked will not *always* have ease. Ahead, there is only eternal life or eternal death. Which would we rather have—a few minutes of fame and glamour, or an eternity of the very best that God has to offer? Can we not journey with the Lord no matter what situations or difficulties He wants to lead us through, knowing that awaiting us is a permanent, glorious, and solid reward?

Can I not hear Him say: *Cynthia, they will reimburse you for your other ticket; buy a one-way ticket home. You have a lot to contend with now—I just need to remind you that you have a great tendency to live life in your own strength. I want to be your Rock, your Fortress, your Deliverer during this particularly stressful time. I don't want you to forget that you need Me.*

Can I not hear Him say: *And Cynthia, for now, your little closet is quite adequate. My plan for you at this time is not to be home much anyway. You need a small home so that you can be free to travel. Also, I always want you to remember that this home is only temporary. There is an eternal home waiting for you, and I know you will like it!*

"But we are citizens of heaven, where the Lord Jesus Christ lives," Paul wrote in his epistle. "And we are eagerly waiting for him to return as our Savior" (Phil. 3:20 NLT). We have to be constantly reminded that this is not our home; we are *in* this world but not *of* it. Consider the story of an older missionary couple returning to America. They happened to be sailing across the Atlantic on the same ship as President Teddy Roosevelt. As they were pulling into New York Harbor, there were bands, flags, and hundreds of people assembled to greet the president. The husband turned to his wife and said, "You know, we served God all of our lives, and we're returning home, and there is no one to greet us." His wife lovingly replied, "But, dear, we are not home yet."

"In what ways are you looking forward to heaven?"

What on Earth Are Heavenly Things?

In Colossians 3:1–4, Paul redirects our focus from the temporal to the eternal:

> If you are then raised up with Christ, reach out for the highest gifts of Heaven, where Christ reigns in power. Be concerned with the heavenly things, not with the passing things of earth. For, as far as this world is concerned, you are already dead, and your true life is a hidden one in God, through Christ. (PHILLIPS)

Since this world is not our home, we need to focus on heavenly things. What are the eternal realities that should be our focus?

First, *God Himself is eternal*. He is from everlasting to everlasting, the Alpha and the Omega. He is to be our main concern. We are to seek *first* His kingdom and His righteousness (Matt. 6:33). That is why the journey to His heart is a worthy destination—God's heart is eternal. He is our Savior, our sovereign Lord, our Guide, our Comforter. There is no other deserving of our wholehearted devotion. In my life, He is my priority. I spend time with Him daily. I walk with Him throughout the day, maintaining a running conversation. I pray that He will always be my first love.

Why is it so important to discern between what is eternal and what is temporal? So that when we are faced with a choice between them, we may choose the eternal first.

Second, *the Word of God endures forever:* "Heaven and earth will disappear, but my words will remain forever" (Matt. 24:35 NLT). The Word speaks to our hearts—teaching, reproving, correcting, and training us. It is powerful and penetrates our thoughts and intentions. It is a book for all times and for all people. It is the only eternal book, and it should hold high priority in our lives. I love the Word of God. It feeds me, enlightens me, and corrects me. It is always fresh. It is one of the best ways to hear God speak. Spending my life enjoying this book has been an incredible blessing in my life.

> *Knowing I will stand before God and answer for how I have spent my life motivates me to live a life that pleases Him.*

Third, *people are eternal.* There is life after this life—either eternal life or eternal punishment (Matt. 25:31–46). Because people are eternal, they, too, are a worthy investment of our lives. Husbands and children are given to us to minister to for eternity. Those who are not married can minister to their immediate families or close friends. I need to be light and salt to neighbors, to friends, to the church, or to anyone to whom God calls me or whom He brings across my path. I have invested the majority of my life in my family. At this time, God has led me to serve as an older woman who encourages other women in their walk with the Lord.

Why is it so important to discern between what is eternal and what is temporal? So that when we are faced with a choice between them, we may choose the eternal first. The other day I had planned to write all day. A friend called and wanted to come over. She knew my schedule but needed to visit for a few minutes. I thought, *The writing is temporary; she is eternal.* Yes, please come over. I want to choose the eternal because I know that one day I will answer for my choices.

"How are your priorities based on what is eternal?"

Giving an Account

Paul describes the coming day when we will appear before the Lord: "For every one of us will have to stand without pretence before Christ our judge, and we shall each receive our due for what we did when we lived in our bodies, whether it was good or bad" (2 Cor. 5:10 PHILLIPS).

Knowing I will stand before God and answer for how I have spent my life motivates me to live a life that pleases Him. It encourages me to choose the eternal. I don't think I can tell God that I just didn't have enough hours in the day to spend with Him. I don't want to look into His face and be ashamed that I was not a student of His Word. I will not be able to say that if I'd had a bigger house, I would have been much more pleasant. I will not say, "Well, Lord, Your grace was just not sufficient for me." I want to have an answer for Him if He asks, "Did you love your neighbor?" The desire of my heart is to hear, "Well done, My good and faithful servant" (Matt. 25:21 NLT).

And so, Peter says, "Remember that the heavenly Father to whom you pray has no favorites when he judges. He will judge or reward you according to what you do. So you must live in reverent fear of him during your time as foreigners here on earth" (1 Peter 1:17 NLT).

Desiring Only God

After Asaph realized that he had been "foolish and ignorant" (Ps. 73:22) in envying the wicked and that God was always with him, guiding him to a "glorious destiny" (v. 24), he could only cry out that God, and God alone, was all he desired. The lifestyles of the rich and famous no longer tempted him, for now he viewed life from God's perspective. He finally comprehended that God was enough, and that He was there to guide and strengthen him to his "glorious destiny." All that mattered was his God:

> Whom have I in heaven but you?
> I desire you more than anything on earth.
> My health may fail, and my spirit may grow weak,
> but God remains the strength of my heart;
> he is mine forever. (Ps. 73:25–26 NLT)

"Do you tell God how much you desire
Him above all else?"

This is my favorite passage in all the Scriptures. I identify so much with Asaph. It is easy for me to want to live for the temporal, for what will satisfy my flesh. I want to desire God more than anything on earth. I want Him to be my portion forever.

And so, dear friend, are you living for the eternal? Should there be some rearranging in your life so that the temporary does not consume all of your time? Have you made the sovereign Lord your shelter? Will you hear, "Well done, my good and faithful servant"? Do you desire God more than anything on earth?

One of the joys of the journey is the freedom to loosen your grasp on the world and focus your energies on what is on God's heart. It makes for a light burden, a strong heart, and an extraordinarily significant life. Consider praying with Peter Marshall:

> Forbid it, Lord, that our roots become too firmly attached to this earth, that we should fall in love with things. Help us to understand that the pilgrimage of this life is but an introduction, a preface, a training school for what is to come. Then shall we see all of life in its true perspective. Then shall we not fall in love with the things of time, but come to love the things that endure.[4]

Not for ease or worldly pleasure
Nor for fame my prayer shall be;
Gladly will I toil and suffer,
Only let me walk with Thee.[5]

TWENTY-THREE

Bringing God Glory

What does it mean to glorify God? It does not
mean to make him more glorious. It means to
acknowledge his glory, and to value it above all
things, and to make it known. . . . Deep within
us we all know that it is our duty to glorify our
Maker by thanking him for all we have, trusting
him for all we need, and obeying all his revealed
will.

John Piper[1]

I have given many people standing ovations to communicate that I
thought they did a remarkable job and that their work was a blessing.
When we receive benefit from others' gifts or from their labor on our
behalf, it's natural to respond by expressing gratitude and offering praise.

I remember feeling this way about a particular tour guide who han-
dled our trip exceptionally well. She cleared away several potential roadblocks and seemed eager to ensure that we were having an enjoyable time.
She even made an extra special effort to get us into a certain landmark
that had been closed. Another time she endured verbal abuse from an
elderly Chinese woman for taking foreigners into the Forbidden City. By

the time we finished our tour, she deserved a standing ovation. We all gave her many thanks, hugs, and gifts for her hard work.

> *We work very hard so that people will praise us. This is living in order to bring ourselves glory.*

If we feel this way for people, how much more conscious we should be of praising "the LORD Almighty—he is the King of glory" (Ps. 24:10 NLT). He is the One who does all things well, who never slumbers or sleeps, who guides us with His gaze fixed constantly upon us. As the journey brings us joy, we will naturally want to bring God glory. And giving God glory sums up the purpose of our lives.

When We Seek to Glorify Ourselves

"Beware of practicing your righteousness before men to be noticed by them," Jesus warned. "Otherwise you have no reward with your Father who is in heaven" (Matt. 6:1 NASB). Many of us go through life intent on making sure that we are recognized and appreciated. We want to be significant and respected. We work very hard so that people will praise us. This is living in order to bring ourselves glory.

Often when I attend a retreat, the head of the committee acknowledges all those who have served. Invariably, someone is left out. Either her name was omitted from the program, or she was not mentioned publicly. I always wonder how that person feels. If she was serving the Lord, then she can acknowledge any hurt feelings without allowing them to change how and why she continues to serve. If she was practicing her righteousness before people, she will nurse that sting and perhaps even distance herself from the group to seek recognition elsewhere. As Oswald Chambers observed, "It is only possible to be humiliated when we are serving our own pride."[2]

Years ago I was attending the annual Christian Booksellers Convention, held each year in July at a major city. My Bible study *Becoming a Woman of Excellence* was at the time listed in the top ten paperback books based on the number of copies sold. The publisher told me that I would be interviewed and specified when I was to be at the booth.

I was there at the appointed time. The woman who came to speak with me looked very official. Her first question was, "Tell me about your book."

"Well, it's really not a book," I replied. "It's a Bible study." The woman looked at me, thought a moment, and said, "Oh, if it isn't a book, then we don't need to have an interview." She turned around and left.

I was new to all this, and I wasn't sure how to respond. I thought, *Well, Lord, it isn't a book. And if Bible studies don't get acknowledged, so be it.* It was a valuable lesson for me. I learned from the beginning that I am not to expect recognition, and I thank the Lord for it. (I have spent many years saying, "It's not a book; it's a Bible study!")

In my T-shirt sightings I spied one that read, "Please don't treat me any differently than you would the queen." I love it! How easy it is to feel offended when we are not treated like royalty!

During the multiple retreats and seminars I have attended, I have slept in every conceivable place and bed. Beds in trailers, beds in dorms, beds in suites, beds in homes, beds in cabins. At times I think, *Lord, I'm the speaker—I deserve the best.* The Lord replies, *Oh, really? Are servants above their Master? Remember, I had no place to lay My head. You are My servant, and you need not be concerned about pillows and beds.* (Although I am tempted, I will not buy that T-shirt!)

Someone who lives to bring herself glory . . .

* wants to be in control.
* seeks to be the center of attention.
* is preoccupied with making sure she receives credit.
* uses her position to achieve recognition.

When the popular song "I Did It My Way" was getting plenty of airtime, I thought that I would hate to stand before God and say, "Lord, I did it my way. I did everything I could so that I was always pleased, and so that people knew who I was. And if they didn't appreciate me, I just left!" When our service starts becoming a performance, and people start becoming our audience, we should see the red flag fluttering; we are seeking to bring glory to ourselves instead of to the One who deserves it. There will be no real joy in the journey when we go down this road.

———

"Where are you tempted to bring glory to self instead of God?"

———

When We Glorify Others

"I am the LORD; that is my name! I will not give my glory to anyone else. I will not share my praise with carved idols," God declared (Isa. 42:8 NLT). Self-seeking is not the only way we violate this truth. When we shift onto others what is rightfully given only to God, we are living to bring other people glory.

The most graphic example of this illicit glorification is the phenomenon of cults. When an individual joins a cult, he commits his life—whether directly or indirectly—to bringing glory to its leader. I read about one group that sells the leader's used bathwater to its members. All cult rulers are, in various ways, worshiped and obeyed. We are painfully aware that the drive to glorify them may even lead to the ultimate sacrifice of members' lives. How tragic to live your life deifying another human!

Belonging to a cult represents the extreme manifestation of this sin, but there are more subtle ways of glorifying others. I have met women who idolize their husbands. By idolize, I mean that a wife in effect worships her husband. He means more to her than her Lord. Her whole life revolves around her mate. A woman who lives this way is so devastated when her husband dies or decides to leave the marriage that after a natural grieving period, she simply feels unable to go on with her life.

Spouses are not the only potential idols near at hand. Some mothers live to bring glory to their children. I met a dear woman whose whole life is centered in her children's activities and accomplishments. Every time you talk with her (I should say "listen to her"), her whole conversation is filled with her children's awards and talents. Her children are her life, and she lives so that she can reflect their glory.

For some women, the temptation to idolatry lies not with children or spouses but in undue commitment to a cause. This woman derives her identity and value solely from what she accomplishes for an organization. The group she is involved in becomes her life, many times to the neglect of her close personal relationships and her walk with God. It is likely a good cause, but it consumes her whole life with efforts to bring money, recognition, and glory to a socially acceptable group, not to God. Indeed, any group, person, or thing to whom we grant illegitimate primacy in our lives can take the place of the Lord.

Whether we seek to glorify ourselves or others, such reverence is misdirected. There is a third option for where we direct our ultimate praise in life, and it is the best!

―――――

"Where are you tempted to glorify another person in place of God?"

―――――

When We Glorify God

Paul clearly and simply states our purpose: "Whatever you eat or drink or whatever you do, you must do all for the glory of God" (1 Cor. 10:31 NLT).

I selected this verse in Corinthians to meditate on for a year. Every day I prayed for God to show me how to bring Him glory, and to show me what I did that did not bring Him glory. It was a painful but profound year in my life.

Halfway through that year, I spoke at a conference with another speaker. The morning the conference began, my talk came first. I shared my message, prayed, and sat down. Everyone was quiet during and after I spoke. We enjoyed a coffee break, and then it was time for the next session and speaker. When this particular woman came to the podium and began to speak, we were all immediately captivated. She was an excellent communicator and extremely humorous. Soon we all had tears of laughter rolling down our faces. When she finished, she deservedly received a standing ovation. As I stood for her and clapped, I began to pray.

Cynthia: Lord, I don't think I should be speaking anymore. I mean, this woman can really *connect* with an audience. She is dynamic. Lord, I'm not like that. In fact, I've never received a standing ovation!

The Lord: Cynthia, if I want one of My servants to receive a standing ovation, that is My concern, not yours.

Cynthia: Yes, Lord.

The Lord: Besides, I thought you were working on My receiving glory.

Cynthia: Yes, I was, but I'm reconsidering all that!

The Lord: Cynthia, this is what it means to bring Me glory—you desire only My glory; you have no concern or question about your glory.

How I love the Lord for teaching me so well the meaning of my verse for that year. It could not have been clearer. We live to call attention to Him, not ourselves.

Why does God want us to bring Him glory? Because He is the only One worthy of receiving glory. Our fulfillment comes in living to exalt Him, for He is our Creator and our sovereign Lord. We spend our lives in vain if we worship anyone else.

> *The difference between the Pharisee and the true disciple is that the Pharisee serves in order to be noticed; the true disciple serves in order that God might be noticed.*

When we come to the end of our lives, we will be empty if all we have cared about is promoting ourselves. If we have spent our lives adoring another human being, who is imperfect and who will die just as we will, we will have only loneliness and heartache. But if we have lived to the glory of God—who is eternal, who will never leave us, and who loves us perfectly—then we will have joy and the gratification of a life well lived.

"Is there an area of your life in which you need to surrender your personal agenda and seek God's glory?"

Living to honor the Lord generates hope: the great expectation of continuing to serve the God we have loved here on earth. There is no end to our delight in declaring with the psalmist, "He is the King of glory" (24:10 NLT). Spurgeon commented on this final verse:

> The closing note is inexpressibly grand. Jehovah of hosts, Lord of men and angels, Lord of the universe, Lord of the worlds, is the King of Glory. All true glory is concentrated upon the true God, for all other glory is but a passing pageant, the painted pomp of an hour. The ascended Savior is here declared to be the Head and Crown of the universe, the King of Glory. Our Immanuel is hymned in sublimest strains. Jesus of Nazareth is Jehovah Sabaoth.[3]

Bringing "Great Glory"

"My true disciples produce much fruit. This brings great glory to my Father," Jesus declared (John 15:8 NLT). When our deepest desire is to bring God glory, then everything else in our lives is focused on this one longing. We become His true disciples, who want nothing more than to honor Him by bearing fruit for His praise.

A branch connected to a grapevine produces grapes. A branch that abides in Christ produces Christlikeness. We love, forgive, serve humbly, exercise patience, show kindness, share our lives with others— all because we continually walk with our Lord. We bear fruit that brings "great glory" to God: "So your light is to shine before men, that they may see the good you do and glorify your Father in heaven" (Matt. 5:16 MOFFATT).

How do you know if you are bringing glory to God? Whenever you do something selflessly, God receives glory.

One result of deep abiding, which produces much fruit, is that what we do will attract people not to us but to the Lord. The difference between the Pharisee and the true disciple is that the Pharisee serves in order to be noticed; the true disciple serves in order that God might be noticed. A true disciple is gentle, humble, unpretentious, sensitive, and gracious.

I have a friend who is a true disciple. When she sees a need, she doesn't say, "Let me know if I can help." She helps. I may find a plate of cookies on my porch or a special book we talked about. I receive notes of encouragement from her. When I'm involved in a project, she may call and say, "I'm bringing dinner for you this week—which night is best?" I find myself thanking the Lord for her. She does not bring glory to herself, because her serving is unobtrusive. I see her good works, but I give glory to God.

So how do you know if you are bringing glory to God? Whenever you do something selflessly, God receives glory. You please Him when you give in secret. You bless Him when you continually thank Him for His love, grace, goodness, sovereignty, and comfort. You glorify Him when you walk by faith and trust Him with all your heart. You show Him that you love Him when you choose to obey and abide.

As Chambers observed, this way of life unfolds one day at a time, in the midst of each experience we walk through with the Lord:

> What is my dream of God's purpose? His purpose is that I depend on Him and on His power now. If I can stay in the middle of the turmoil calm and unperplexed, that is the end of the purpose of God. God is not working towards a particular finish; His end is the process—that I see Him walking on the waves, no shore in sight, no success, no goal, just the absolute certainty that it is all right because I see Him walking on the sea. It is the process, not the end, which is glorifying to God.[4]

Jesus prayed to the Father, "I brought glory to you here on earth by doing everything you told me to do" (John 17:4 NLT). Doing everything God asks you to do brings Him great glory. And surrendering all in order to journey to the heart of God brings great blessing, for only in Him will you experience fullness of joy, and only in His right hand will you find everlasting pleasure. To God be all the glory.

Refresh Thy people on their toilsome way,
Lead us from night to neverending day;
Fill all our lives with love and grace divine,
And glory, laud, and praise be ever Thine![5]

The Father
and the Child

The child spoke:

I'm nearing the end of my journey, aren't I,
Father?

*Yes, My child, but there are still a few more roads to
travel.*

It has been a good journey. Thank You for holding my hand.

Have you lacked for anything?

No, nothing. I must confess I was skeptical that
all I needed to take on the journey was a willing
heart. I didn't realize then that when You have
my heart, You are all I ever need or want.

What have you learned from your travels?

I've learned that being a woman who pleases You
has nothing to do with my family, my friends, or
my circumstances, but everything to do with how
much I love You and how deeply I abide in You.

How would you describe your journey?

As a journey that frees me to become all You created me to be—as a journey of great inner Joy.

What have you learned about Joy?

Joy has always been deep in my heart, but she is
quiet. I've learned that I must be still to hear her;
otherwise, I listen to louder voices that silence
hers.

How has Joy served you?

She has faithfully been with me in all of my
journey—my trials, my suffering, my obedience,
and my serving. I understand now that she

always accompanies Sorrow—but her most precious gift to me is her tears as I experience Your presence.

How has Sorrow helped you?

Father, I know I said in the beginning that I didn't want Sorrow to go with me, but she has taught me much. Without her, I would never have wept over my sin. Whenever I was deeply hurt or grieving, she took me straight to Your heart. Without her, I would not have known how others felt. I would not have known how to love or serve them. And as You said, it has been Sorrow that taught me the meaning of true Joy.

And what is true Joy?

True Joy is knowing and experiencing Your heart.

Is there anything you want for the rest of your journey?

In the past, I know I would have had a list, Father. But now, I want only one thing—and that is to bring You glory.

Once more, the child stretched out her hand. The Father, knowing the great love His child had for Him, took her hand, and they continued on their journey.

NOTES

Preface
1. Oswald Chambers, *My Utmost for His Highest* (Westwood, N.J.: Barbour & Co., 1935), Dec. 15.

Chapter 1—Preparing for a Lifetime Journey
1. A. W. Tozer, *The Pursuit of God* (Camp Hill, Penn.: Christian Publications, 1982), 14.
2. William Law, quoted in "Freedom of Surrender," by Gary Thomas, *Discipleship Journal*, 95 (Sept.–Oct. 1996), 54.
3. Chambers, *My Utmost for His Highest,* Sept. 24.
4. Cecil Frances Alexander, "Jesus Calls Us o'er the Tumult," in *Hymns for the Family of God* (Nashville: Paragon Associates, 1976), 399.

Chapter 2—An Invitation
1. John Bunyan, *Pilgrim's Progress* (New York: Penguin, 1965), 24–25.
2. Chambers, *My Utmost for His Highest,* April 6.
3. Eugene H. Peterson, *A Long Obedience in the Same Direction* (Downers Grove: InterVarsity Press, 1980), 29.
4. Horatius Bonar, "I Heard the Voice of Jesus Say," in *Hymns for the Family of God,* 51.

Chapter 3—Relinquish Control
1. Jonathan Edwards, quoted in Edna Gerstner, *Jonathan and Sarah: An Uncommon Union* (Morgan, Penn.: Soli Deo Gloria, 1995), 240.
2. Tozer, *The Pursuit of God,* 104.
3. Judson W. Van de Venter, "I Surrender All," in *Hymns for the Family of God,* 408.

Chapter 4—Faith for the Unforeseen
1. Calvin Miller, *Walking with Saints* (Nashville: Thomas Nelson, 1995), xxii.
2. Chambers, *My Utmost for His Highest,* May 25.
3. Henri J. M. Nouwen, quoted in *A Guide to Prayer for Ministers and Other Servants,* by Rueben P. Job and Norman Shawchuck (Nashville: Upper Room, 1983), 325.
4. F. B. Meyer, quoted in *Streams in the Desert,* ed. Mrs. Charles E. Cowman (Grand Rapids: Zondervan/Daybreak, 1965), 17–18.
5. Edgar P. Stites, "Trusting Jesus," in *Hymns for the Family of God,* 79.

Chapter 5—Travel Light
1. J. R. M., quoted in *Streams in the Desert,* 9.
2. Lawrence O. Richards, *Expository Dictionary of Bible Words* (Grand Rapids: Zondervan, 1985), 291.

3. Corrie Ten Boom, *Clippings from My Notebook* (Minneapolis: World Wide, 1982), 93–94.
4. Brennan Manning, *Abba's Child* (Colorado Springs: NavPress, 1994), 68.
5. Joseph M. Scriven, "What a Friend We Have in Jesus," in *Hymns for the Family of God*, 466.

Chapter 6—Fellowship with Our Guide
1. Charles Stanley, *The Wonderful Spirit-Filled Life* (Nashville: Thomas Nelson, 1992), 88.
2. J. Oswald Sanders, *Enjoying Intimacy with God* (Chicago: Moody, 1980), 71.
3. David Brainerd, *The Life of David Brainerd,* ed. Jonathan Edwards (Grand Rapids: Baker, 1978), 59.
4. Brother Lawrence, "The Practice of the Presence of God," in *The Treasury of Christian Spiritual Classics* (Nashville: Thomas Nelson, 1994), 571, 577.
5. Brainerd, *Life of David Brainerd,* 56, 59.
6. Chambers, *My Utmost for His Highest,* Feb. 21.
7. Ken Gire, *Windows of the Soul* (Grand Rapids: Zondervan, 1996), 36.
8. James G. Small, "I've Found a Friend, O Such a Friend," in *Hymns for the Family of God*, 220.

Chapter 7—The Guidebook
1. Frederick Buechner, *Now and Then* (New York: Harper & Row, 1983), 21.
2. Dietrich Bonhoeffer, quoted in *A Long Obedience in the Same Direction,* 32.
3. Alexander Groves, "Break Thou the Bread of Life," in *Hymns for the Family of God,* 30.

Chapter 8—A Passionate Reverence
1. Francis Davison, quoted in *The Treasury of David,* by Charles Spurgeon, vol. 2 (McLean, Va.: MacDonald, n.d.), 473.
2. Oswald Chambers, *The Oswald Chambers Daily Devotional Bible* (Nashville: Thomas Nelson, 1992), 3.
3. Robert Nisbet, quoted in *Psalms,* by Charles H. Spurgeon, ed. David Otis Fuller (Grand Rapids: Kregel Publications, 1968), 594.
4. Folliott S. Pierpoint, "For the Beauty of the Earth," in *Hymns for the Family of God,* 1.

Chapter 9—Stay on the Path
1. Friedrich Nietzsche, quoted in *A Long Obedience in the Same Direction,* 10.
2. Charles H. Spurgeon, *The Treasury of David,* vol. 2, 341.
3. John E. Bode, "O Jesus, I Have Promised," in *Hymns for the Family of God,* 402.

Chapter 10—Righteous Clothing
1. C. S. Lewis, quoted in *Closer Walk* (Atlanta: Walk Thru the Bible, 1991), Sept. 15.
2. Chambers, *My Utmost for His Highest,* July 9; Oct. 6.
3. Ibid., Dec. 27.

4. William Gurnall, *The Christian in Complete Armour*, vol. 1 (Carlisle, Penn.: The Banner of Truth Trust, 1989), 33.
5. Frederick Temple, quoted in *Joy and Strength*, ed. Mary Wilder Tileston (Minneapolis: World Wide, 1988), 138.
6. William R. Featherston, "My Jesus, I Love Thee," in *Hymns for the Family of God*, 456.

Chapter 11—Wise Traveling Companions

1. Dee Brestin, *The Friendships of Women* (Wheaton: Victor, 1988), 102.
2. Eugene H. Peterson, *Living the Message* (San Francisco: Harper, 1996), 268.
3. Laurence J. Peter, quoted in *From Friend to Friend* (Fort Worth: Brownlow, 1992), 51.
4. Amy Carmichael, *IF* (Grand Rapids: Zondervan, 1965), n.p.
5. John Fawcett, "Blest Be the Tie That Binds," in *Hymns for the Family of God*, 560.

Chapter 12—Willingness to Endure

1. Peterson, *Living the Message*, 271.
2. Gary Inrig, *Quality Friendship* (Chicago: Moody, 1981), 197–98.
3. Amy Carmichael, *Edges of His Ways* (Fort Washington, Penn.: Christian Literature Crusade, 1955), 5.
4. "How Firm a Foundation," in *Hymns for the Family of God*, 32.

Chapter 13—His Immeasurable Love

1. A. W. Tozer, *The Knowledge of the Holy* (San Francisco: Harper, 1961), 104.
2. Julian of Norwich, "Revelations of Divine Love," in *Treasury of Christian Classics*, 343.
3. Chambers, *My Utmost for His Highest*, July 30.
4. C. S. Lewis, quoted in *Insights* magazine (spring 1983), 11.
5. C. S. Lewis, *Mere Christianity* (New York: Macmillan, 1943), 117–18.
6. James G. Small, "I've Found a Friend, O Such a Friend," in *Hymns for the Family of God*, 220.

Chapter 14—His Boundless Grace

1. Donald Barnhouse, quoted in *The Grace Awakening*, by Charles Swindoll (Dallas: Word, 1990), 9.
2. Charles Wesley, "And Can It Be That I Should Gain?" in *Hymns for the Family of God*, 260.
3. W. Grinton Berry, ed., *Foxe's Book of Martyrs* (Grand Rapids: Baker, 1978), 26.
4. Chambers, *Daily Devotional Bible*, 294.
5. Ray Palmer, "My Faith Looks up to Thee," in *Hymns for the Family of God*, 84.

Chapter 15—His Manifold Goodness

1. Matthew Henry, *The Quotable Matthew Henry* (Old Tappan, N.J.: Revell, 1982), 106.
2. Chambers, *My Utmost for His Highest*, May 25.

3. George D. Watson, quoted in *Don't Waste Your Sorrows,* by Paul E. Billheimer (Minneapolis: Bethany, 1977), 76.
4. Fanny J. Crosby, "To God Be the Glory," in *Hymns for the Family of God,* 363.

Chapter 16—His Absolute Sovereignty

1. Lewis Sperry Chafer, *Chafer Systematic Theology.* vol. 1 (Dallas: Dallas Seminary Press, 1947), 215–16.
2. John Dick, quoted in *Chafer Systematic Theology,* 243.
3. Chafer, *Chafer Systematic Theology,* 236.
4. Ibid., 237–38.
5. Chambers, *Daily Devotional Bible,* 140.
6. Maltbie D. Babcock, "This Is My Father's World," in *Hymns for the Family of God,* 6.

Chapter 17—His Perfect Will

1. Chambers, *Daily Devotional Bible,* 175.
2. Chambers, *My Utmost for His Highest,* Jan. 4.
3. Ibid., May 13.
4. Ibid., March 20.
5. Ibid., April 16.
6. Webb-Peploe, quoted in *Coping, Insights from: Amy Carmichael, C. S. Lewis, Charles Spurgeon, Hudson Taylor,* ed. Elizabeth Skoglund (Ventura, Calif.: Regal Books, 1971), 48.
7. Saint Thérèse of Lisieux, in *Prayers Across the Centuries* (Wheaton: Harold Shaw, 1993), 125.
8. Joachim Neander, translated by Catherine Winkworth, "Praise to the Lord, the Almighty," in *Hymns for the Family of God,* 337.

Chapter 18—His Incomparable Ways

1. Katharina von Schlegel, translated by Jane L. Borthwick, "Be Still My Soul," in *Hymns for the Family of God,* 77.
2. J. C. Ryle, quoted in *Closer Walk* (Atlanta: Walk Thru the Bible, 1990), Nov. 8.
3. Gary Thomas, "The Freedom of Surrender," *Discipleship Journal,* no. 95 (Sept.–Oct. 1996), 52.
4. Jerry Bridges, *Trusting God* (Colorado Springs: NavPress, 1988), 175.
5. *Webster's Ninth New Collegiate Dictionary* (Springfield, Mass.: Merriam-Webster, 1981), 412.
6. Francis de Sales, quoted in *Streams in the Desert,* 51.
7. Lina Sandell, translated by A. L. Skoog, "Day by Day and with Each Passing Moment," in *Hymns for the Family of God,* 102.

Chapter 19—His Abundant Comfort

1. Charles H. Spurgeon, *Morning and Evening,* ed. Roy H. Clarke (Nashville: Thomas Nelson, 1994), February 12.
2. Chambers, *My Utmost for His Highest,* June 25.
3. Personal letter from Bea Ann Kangas, 1996, used by permission.
4. Daniel W. Whittle, "Moment by Moment," in *Hymns for the Family of God,* 65.

Chapter 20—Bearing His Fruit

1. Evelyn Underhill, quoted in *A Guide to Prayer for Ministers and Other Servants*, 320.
2. From a quotation attributed to Aristides, documentation unknown.
3. Eugene H. Peterson, *Traveling Light* (Colorado Springs: Helmers & Howard, 1988), 181.
4. Chambers, *My Utmost for His Highest*, Feb. 4.
5. Quoted in an unpublished missionary newsletter from Mark and Maryanna Lanford, 7 September 1993.
6. Fanny J. Crosby, "Redeemed," in *Hymns for the Family of God*, 646.

Chapter 21—Experiencing His Rest

1. Amy Carmichael, *Learning from God*, ed. Stuart and Brenda Blance (Fort Washington, Penn.: Christian Literature Crusade, 1985), 53.
2. Chambers, *My Utmost for His Highest*, Nov. 15.
3. Jerome, quoted in *The Treasury of David*, by Charles Spurgeon, vol. 1 (McLean, Va.: MacDonald, n.d.), 185.
4. A. B. Davidson, quoted in *The Life of Hidden Prayer*, by David M'Intyre (Minneapolis: Bethany, 1993), 31.
5. Charles H. Spurgeon, *The Treasury of David*, vol. 3 (McLean, Va.: MacDonald, n.d.), 137.
6. Frances Ridley Havergal, "Like a River Glorious," in *Hymns for the Family of God*, 497.

Chapter 22—Living for the Eternal

1. Hans Küng, from *On Being a Christian*, quoted in *Disciplines for the Inner Life* (Nashville: Nelson/Generoux, 1989), 384.
2. Carmichael, *Learning from God*, 120.
3. Dan Allender, *Bold Love* (Colorado Springs: NavPress, 1992), 140.
4. Peter Marshall, "Liberation from Materialism," quoted in *Hymns for the Family of God*, 464.
5. Fanny J. Crosby, "Close to Thee," in *Hymns for the Family of God*, 405.

Chapter 23—Bringing God Glory

1. John Piper, *Desiring God* (Portland: Multnomah, 1986), 43–44.
2. Chambers, *Daily Devotional Bible*, 27.
3. Spurgeon, *Treasury of David*, 1:378.
4. Chambers, *My Utmost for His Highest*, July 28.
5. Daniel C. Roberts, "God of Our Fathers," in *Hymns for the Family of God*, 687.